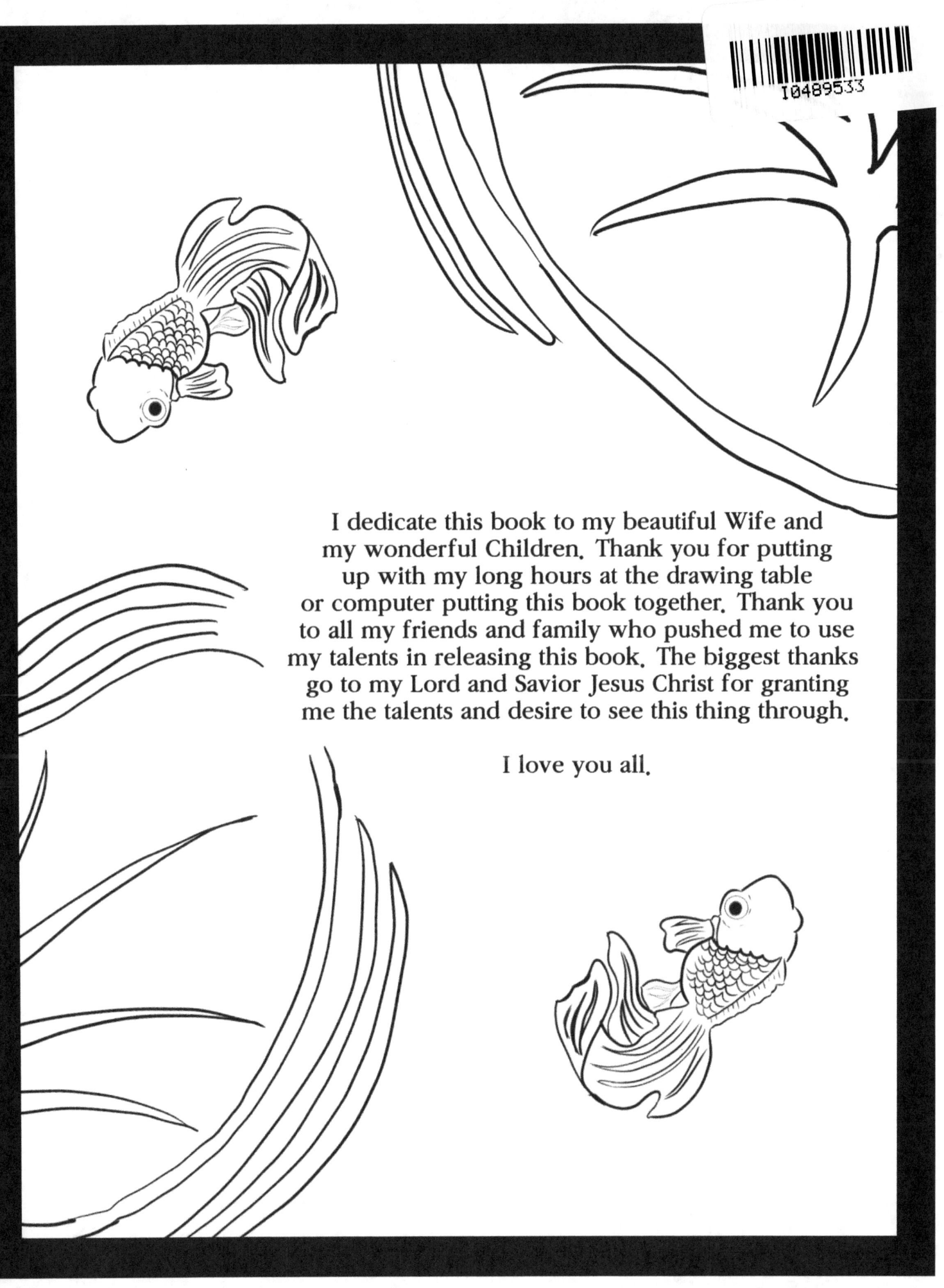

I dedicate this book to my beautiful Wife and
my wonderful Children. Thank you for putting
up with my long hours at the drawing table
or computer putting this book together. Thank you
to all my friends and family who pushed me to use
my talents in releasing this book. The biggest thanks
go to my Lord and Savior Jesus Christ for granting
me the talents and desire to see this thing through.

I love you all.

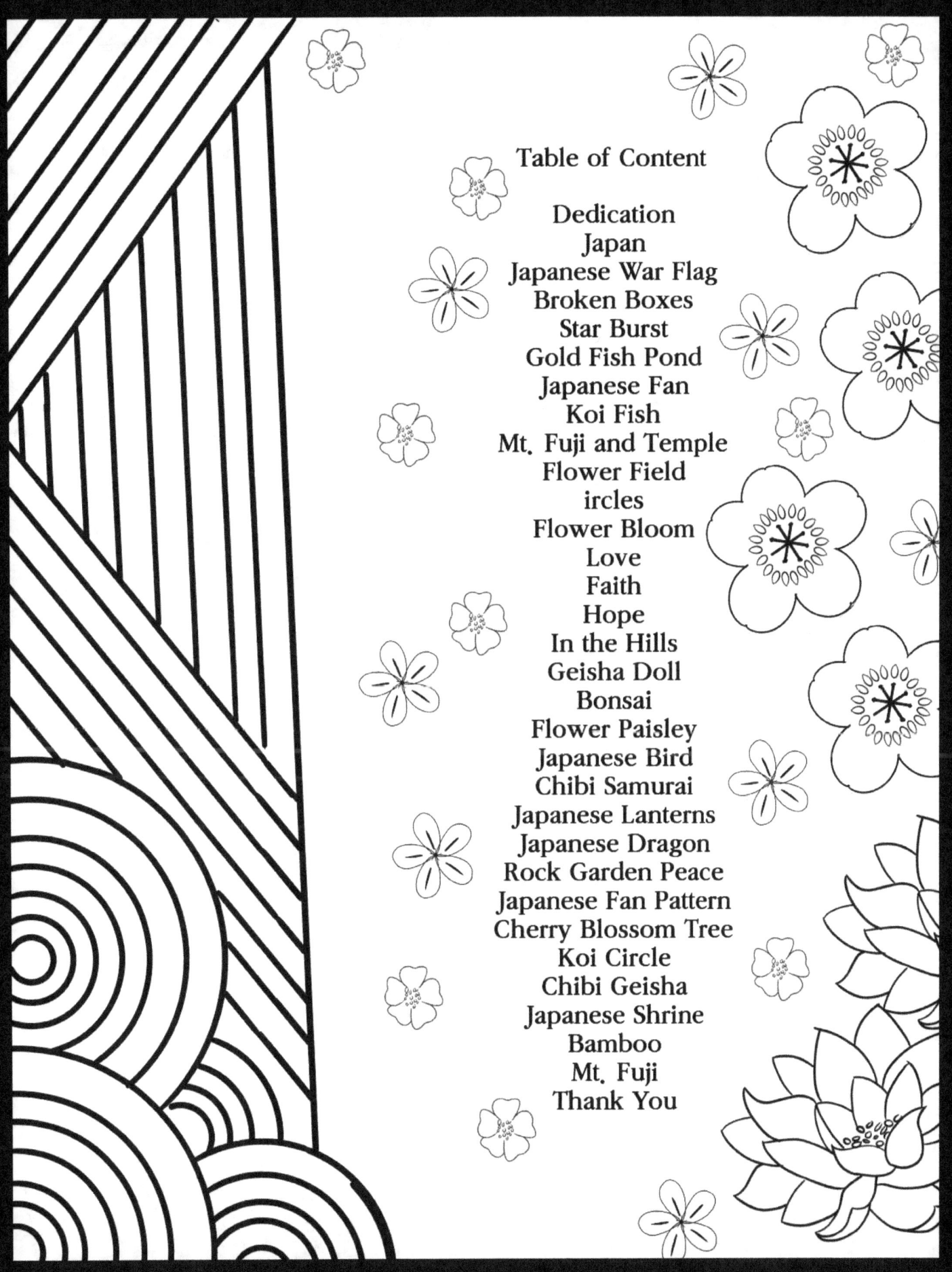

Table of Content

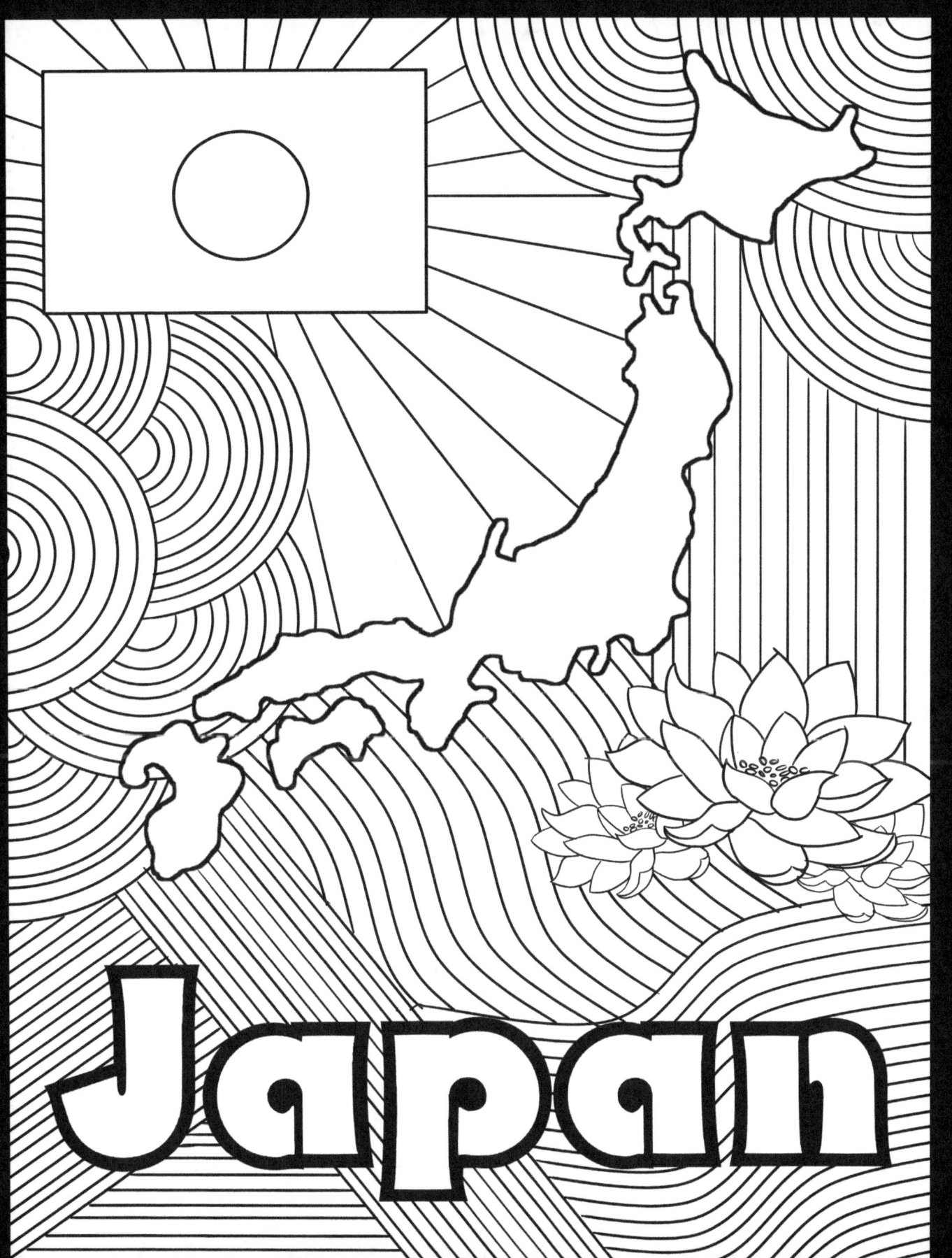

Japan

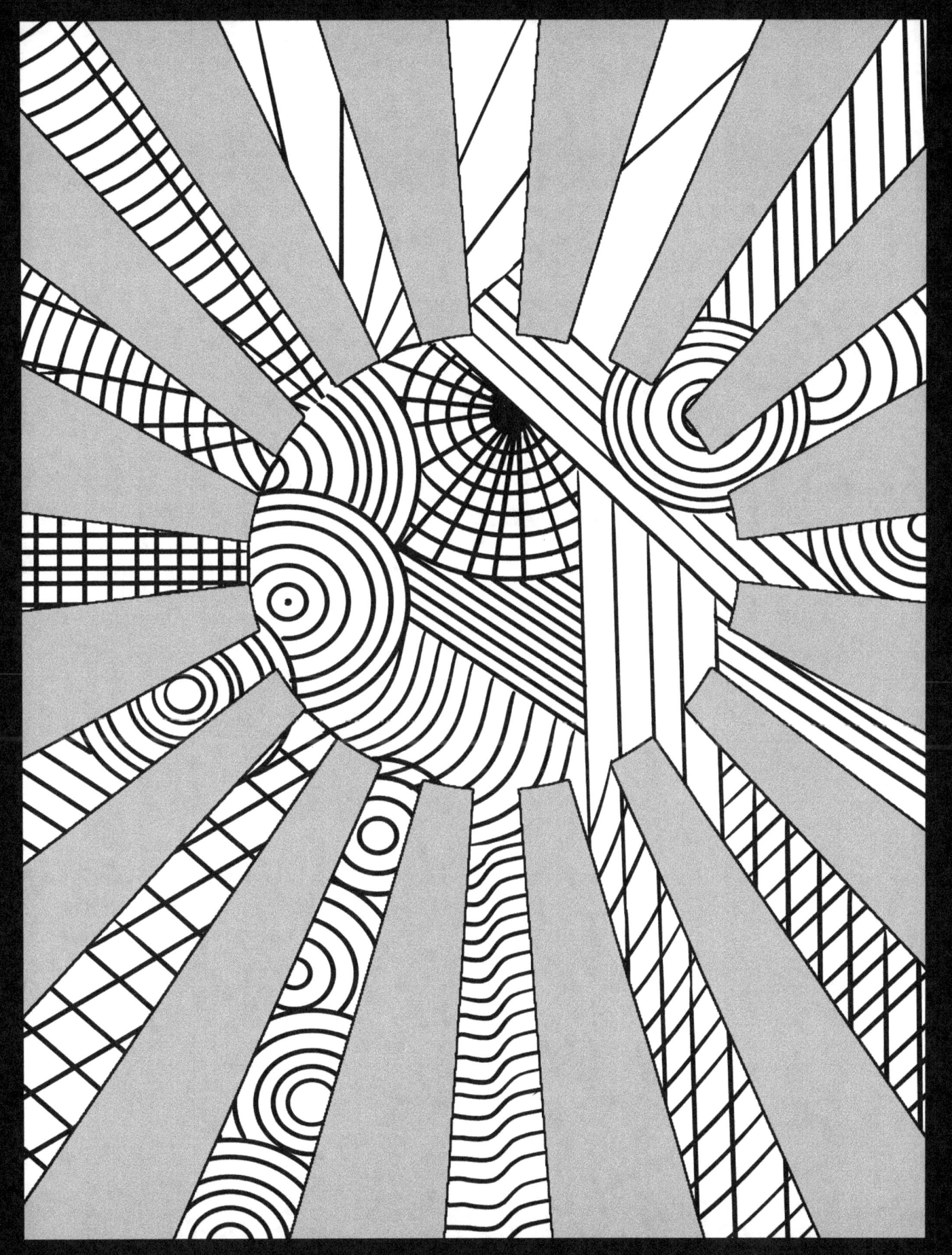

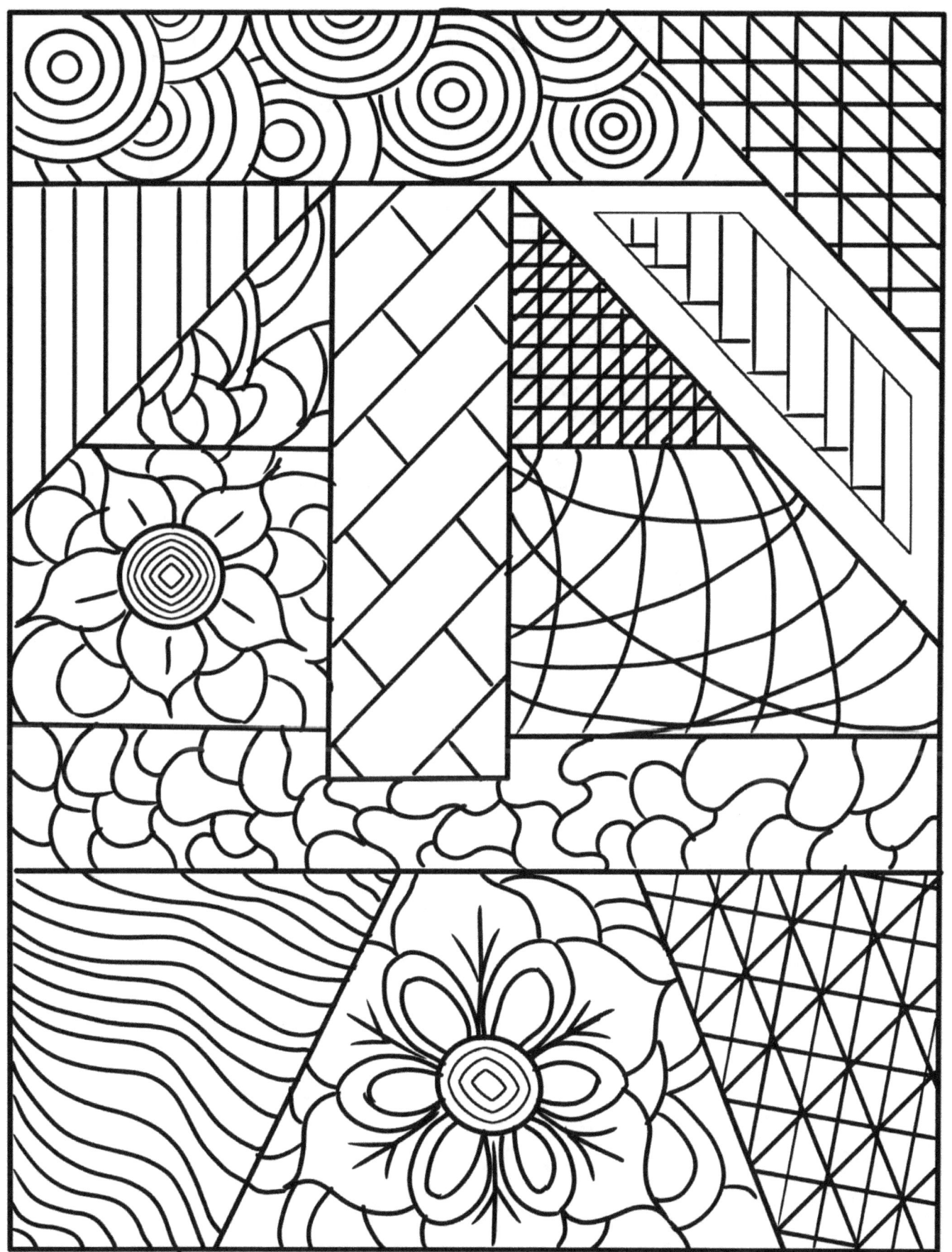

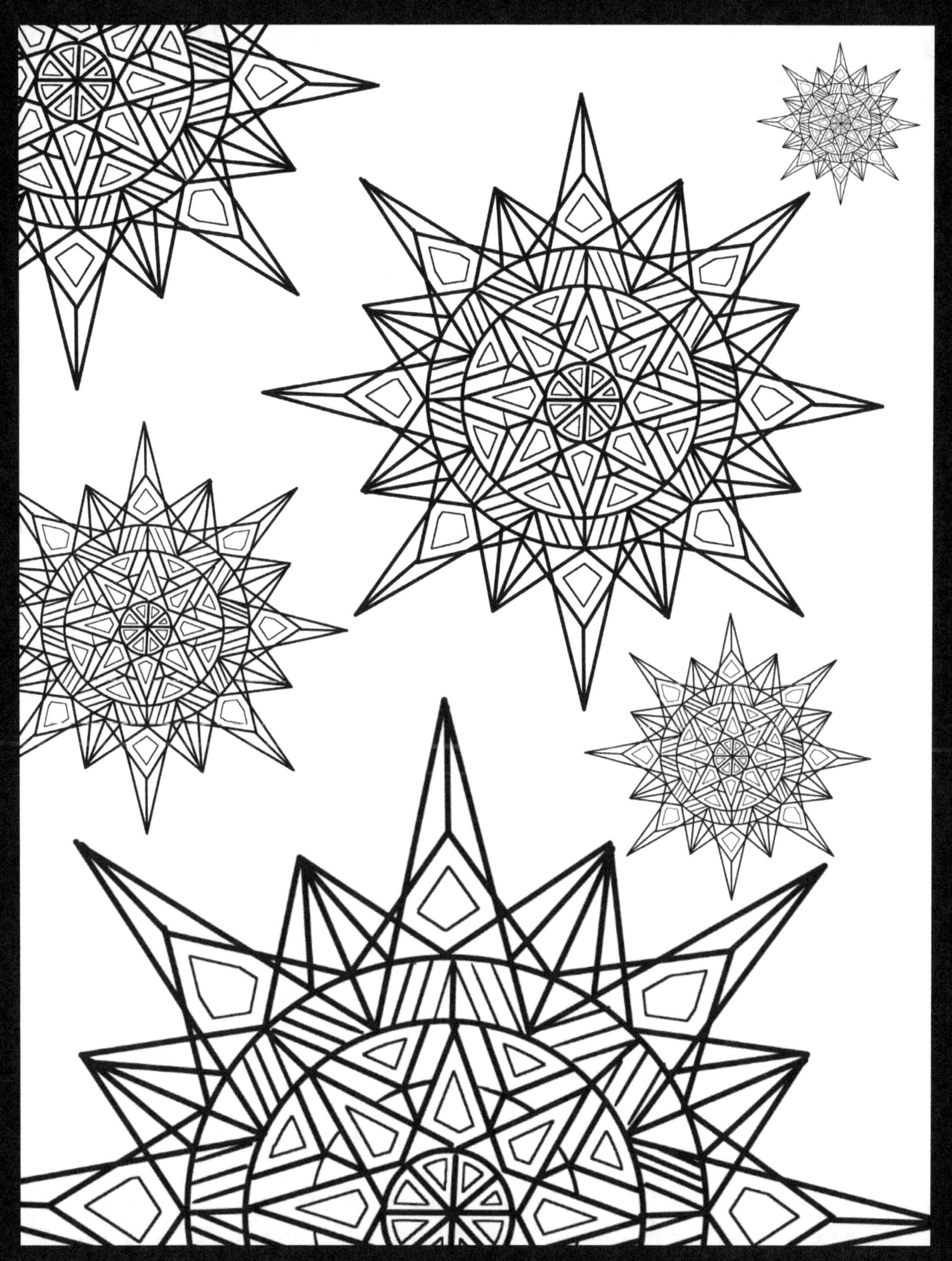

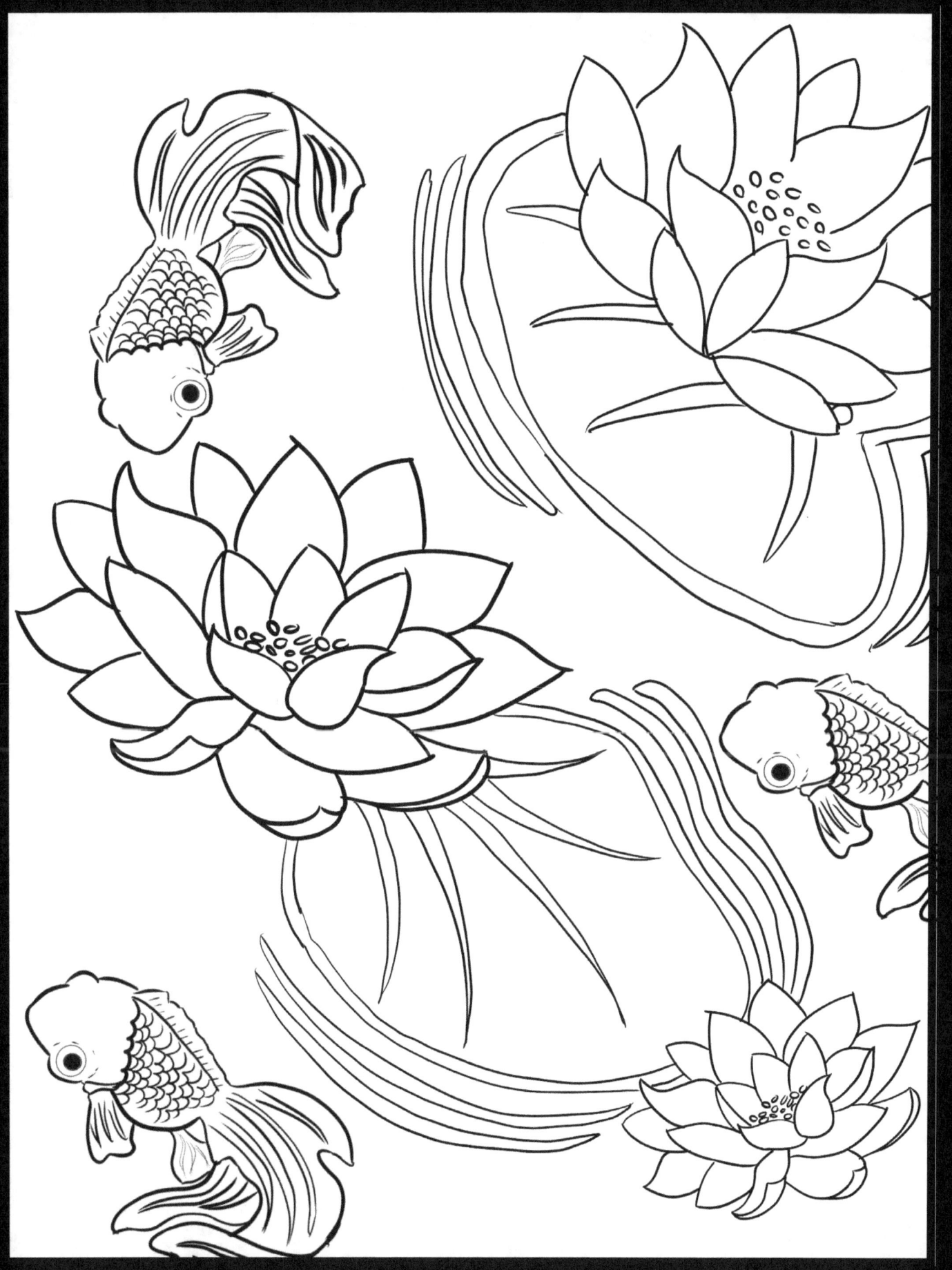

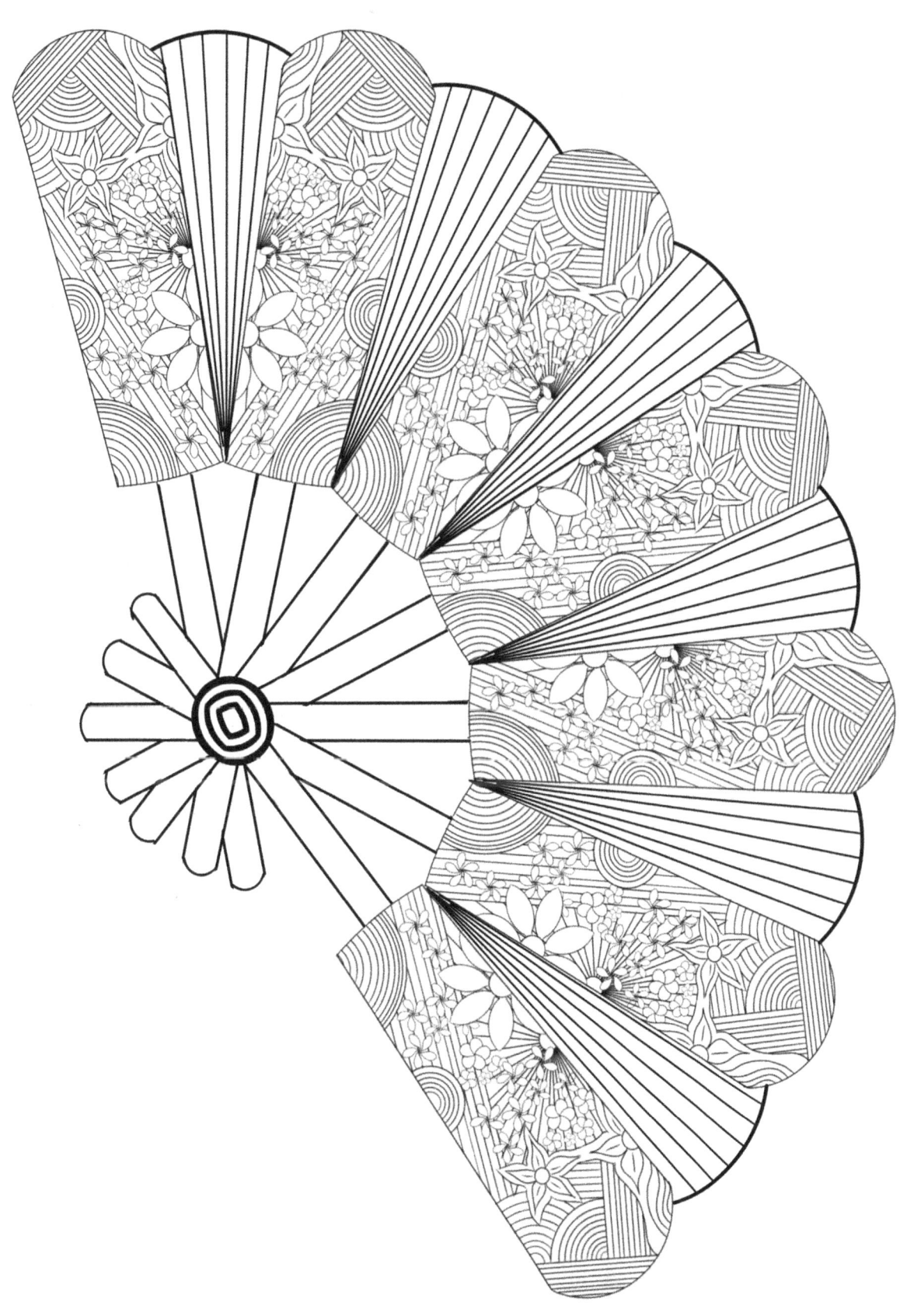

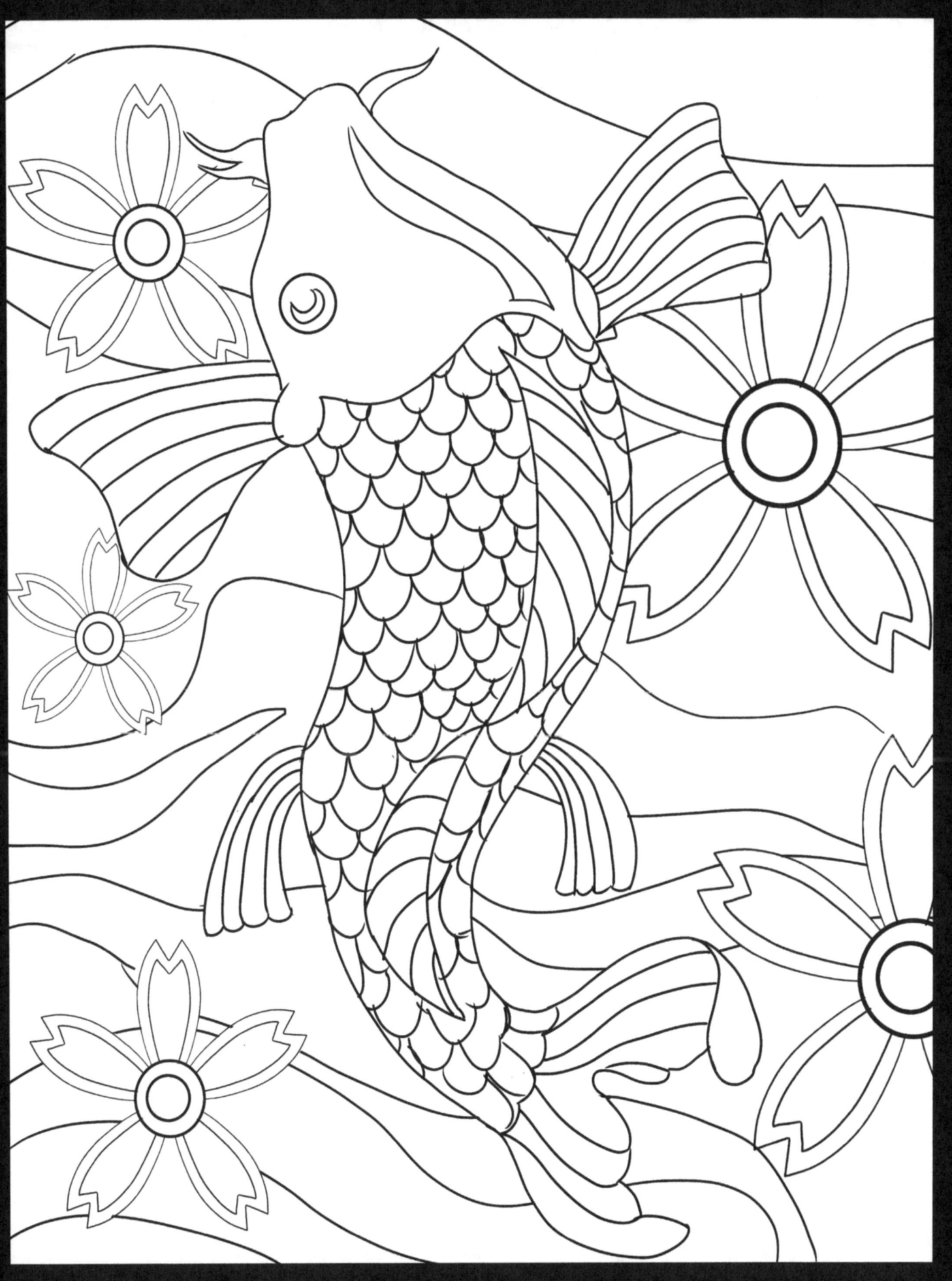

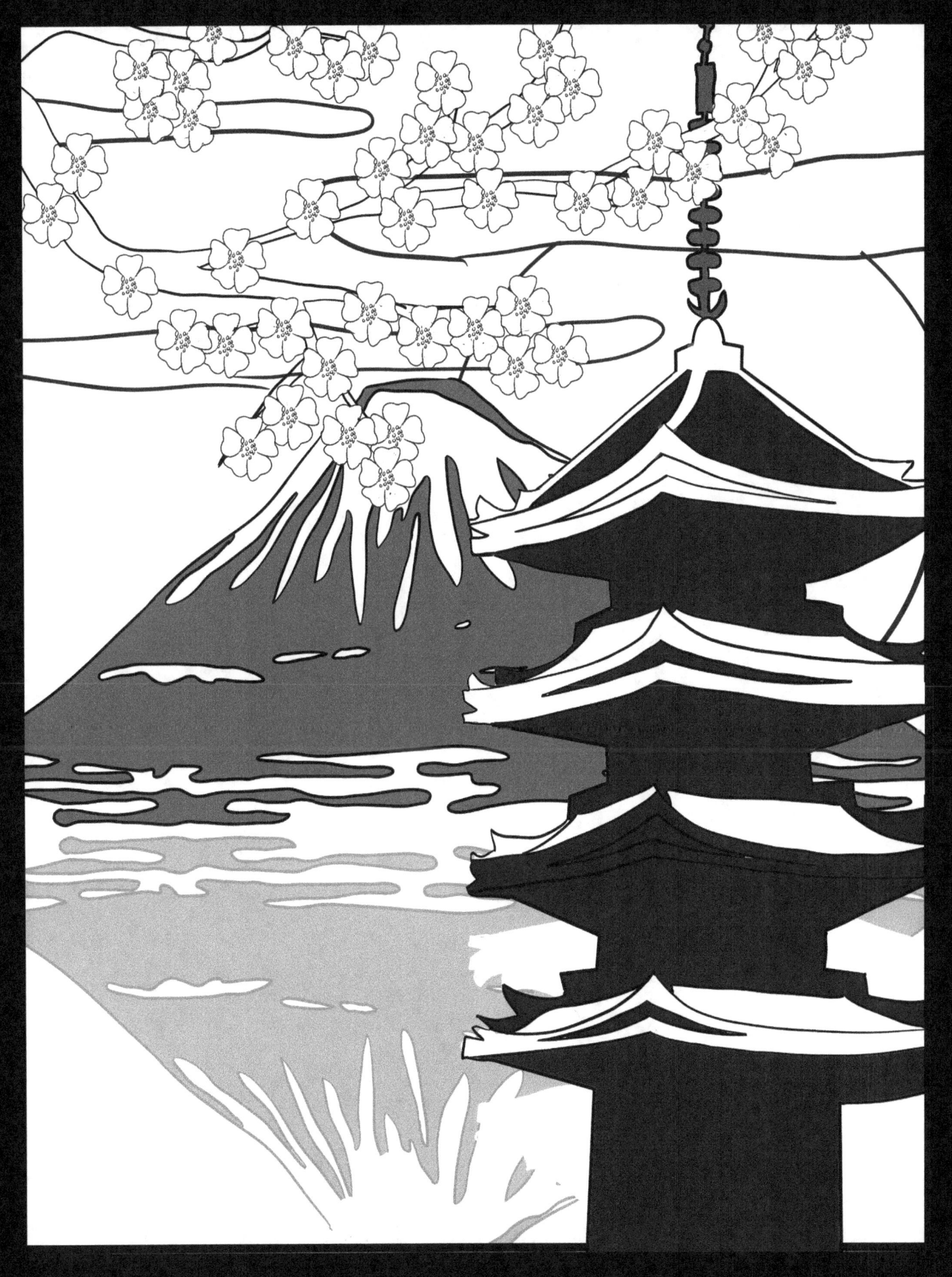

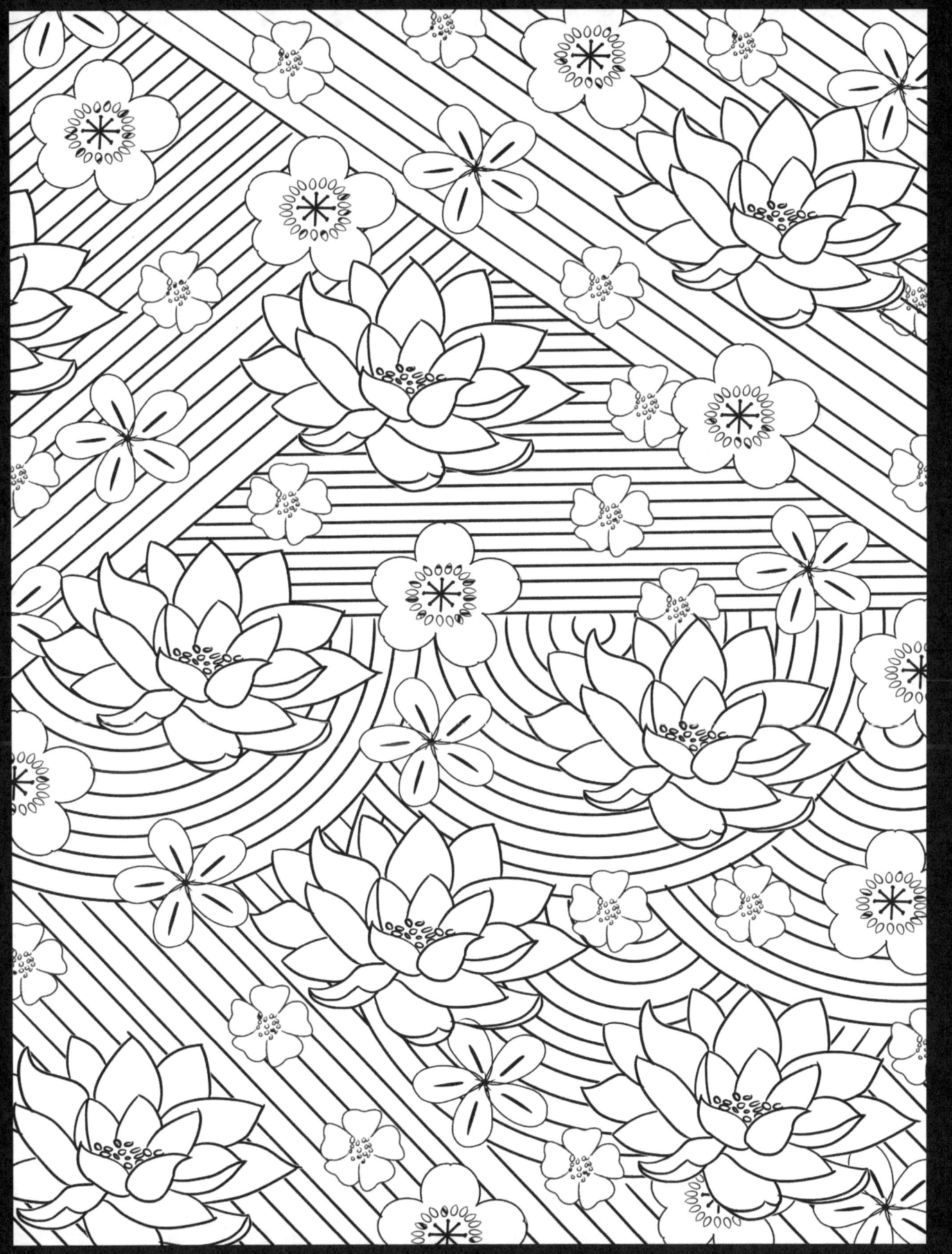

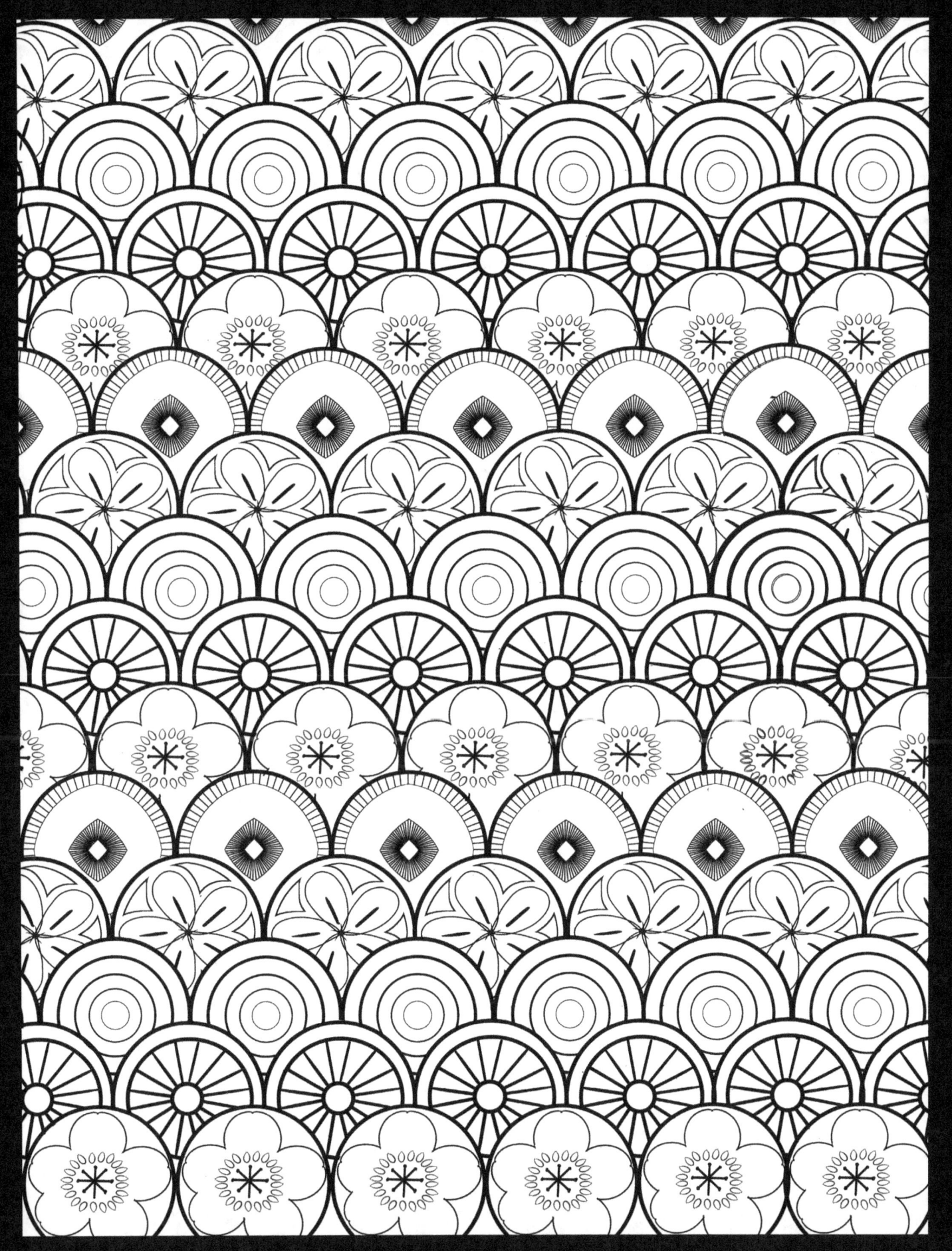

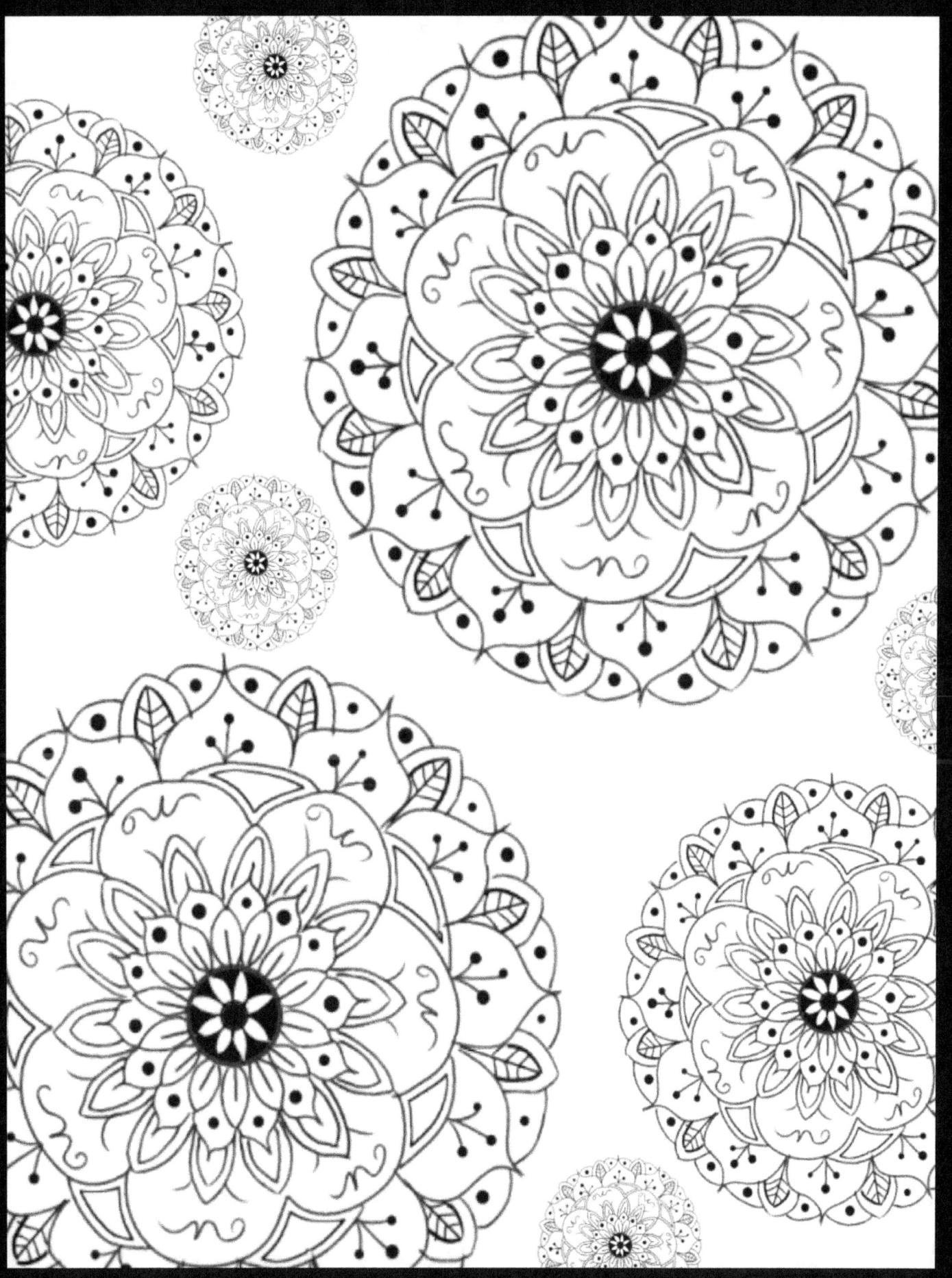

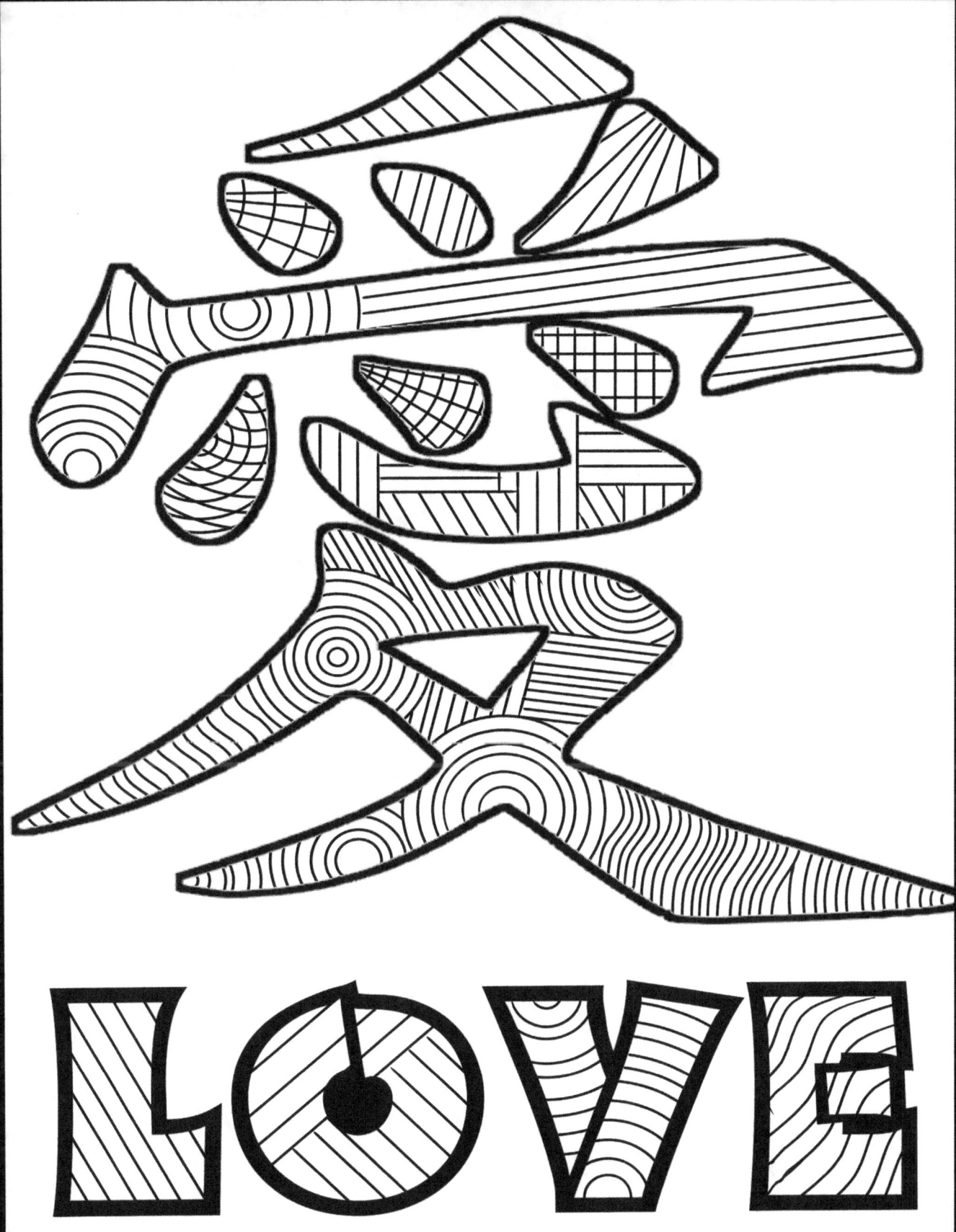

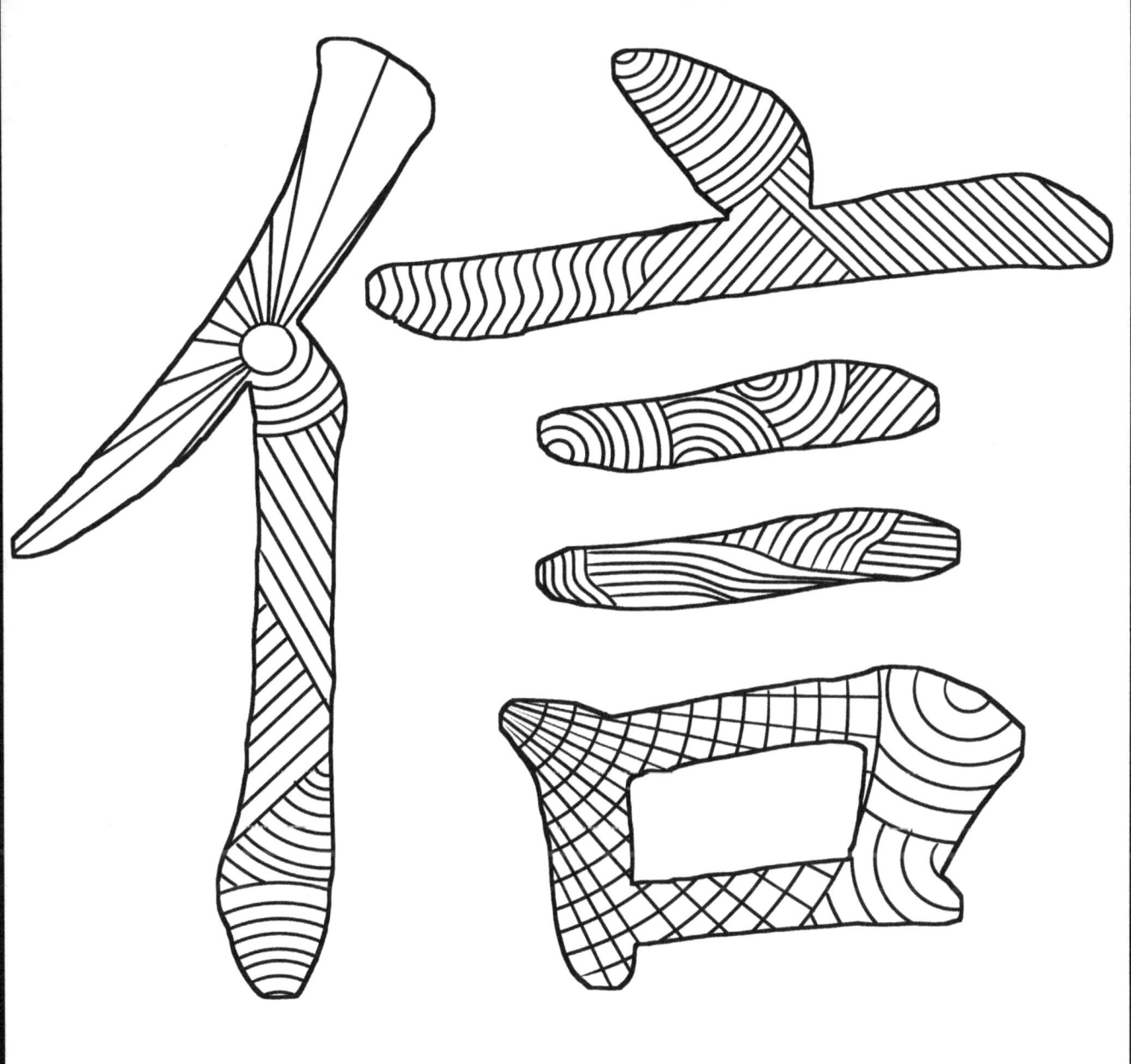

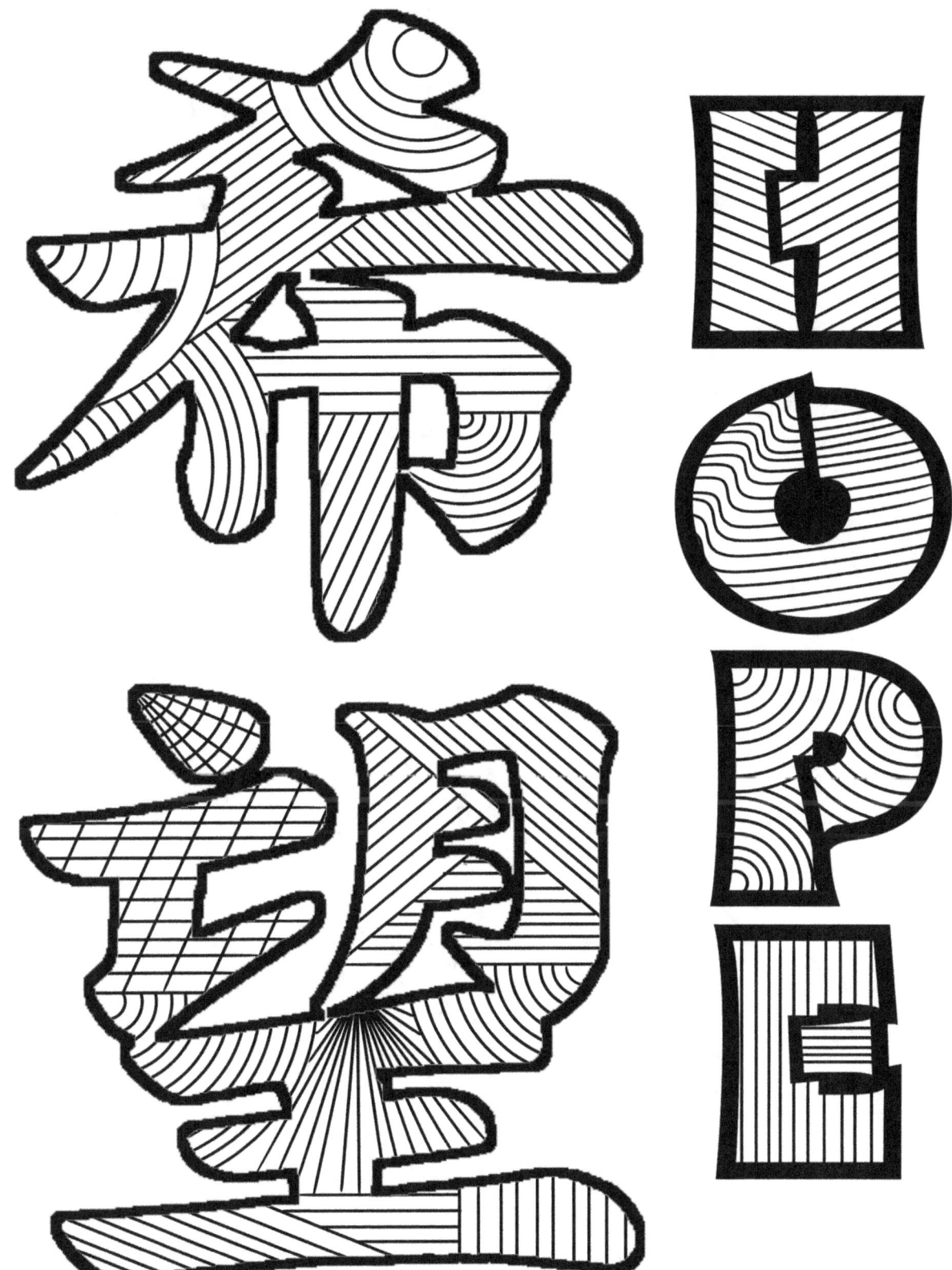

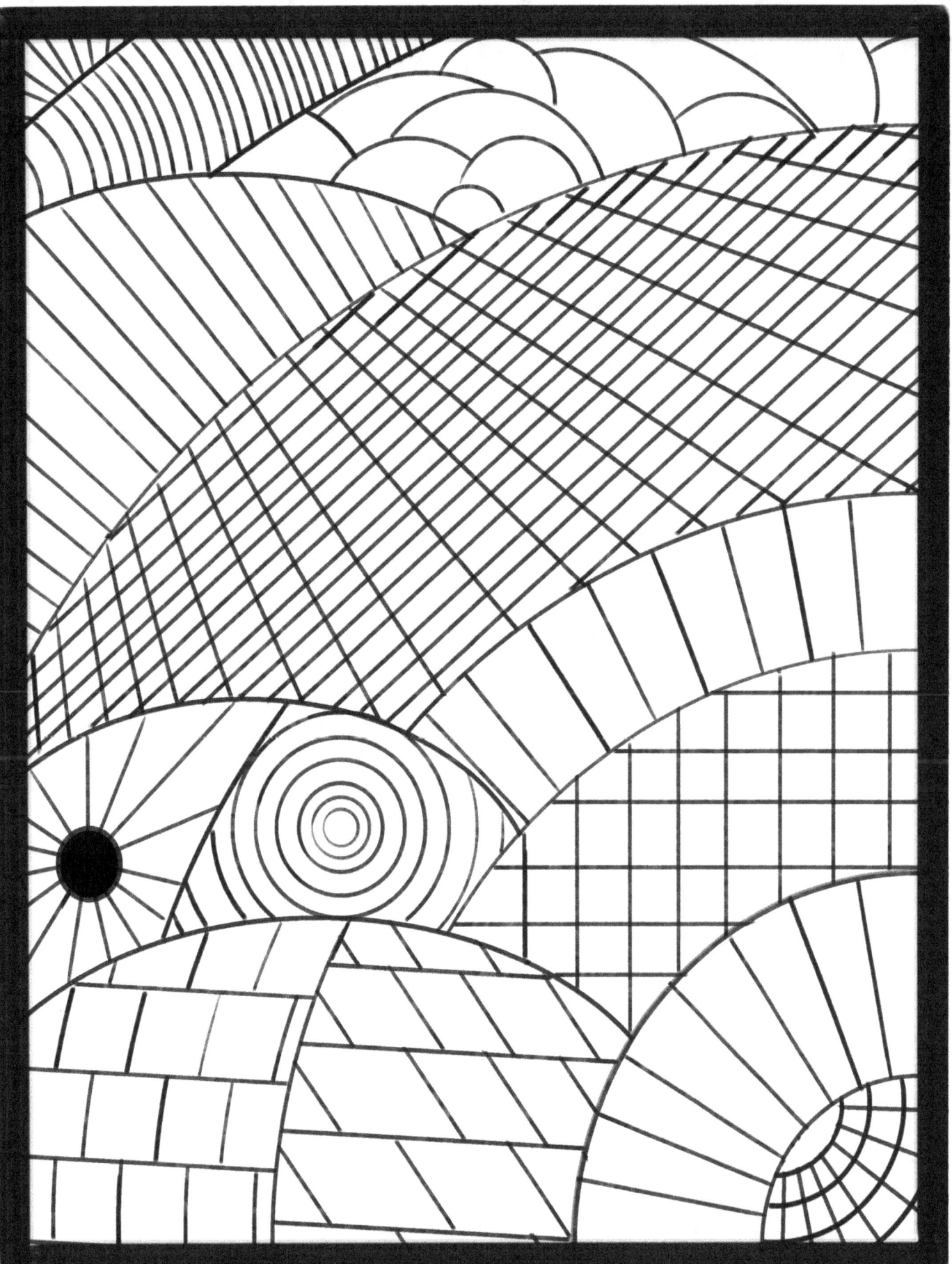

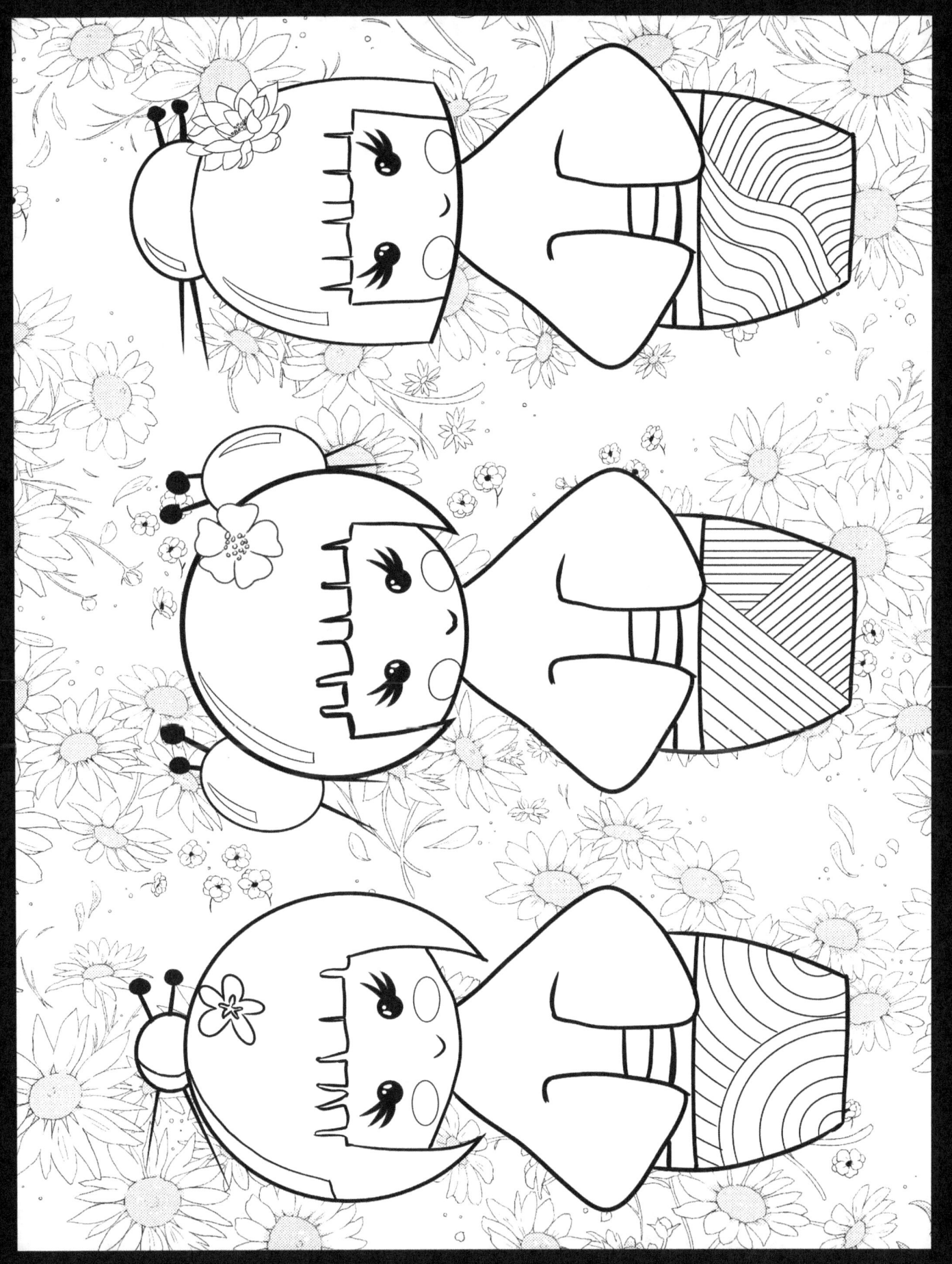

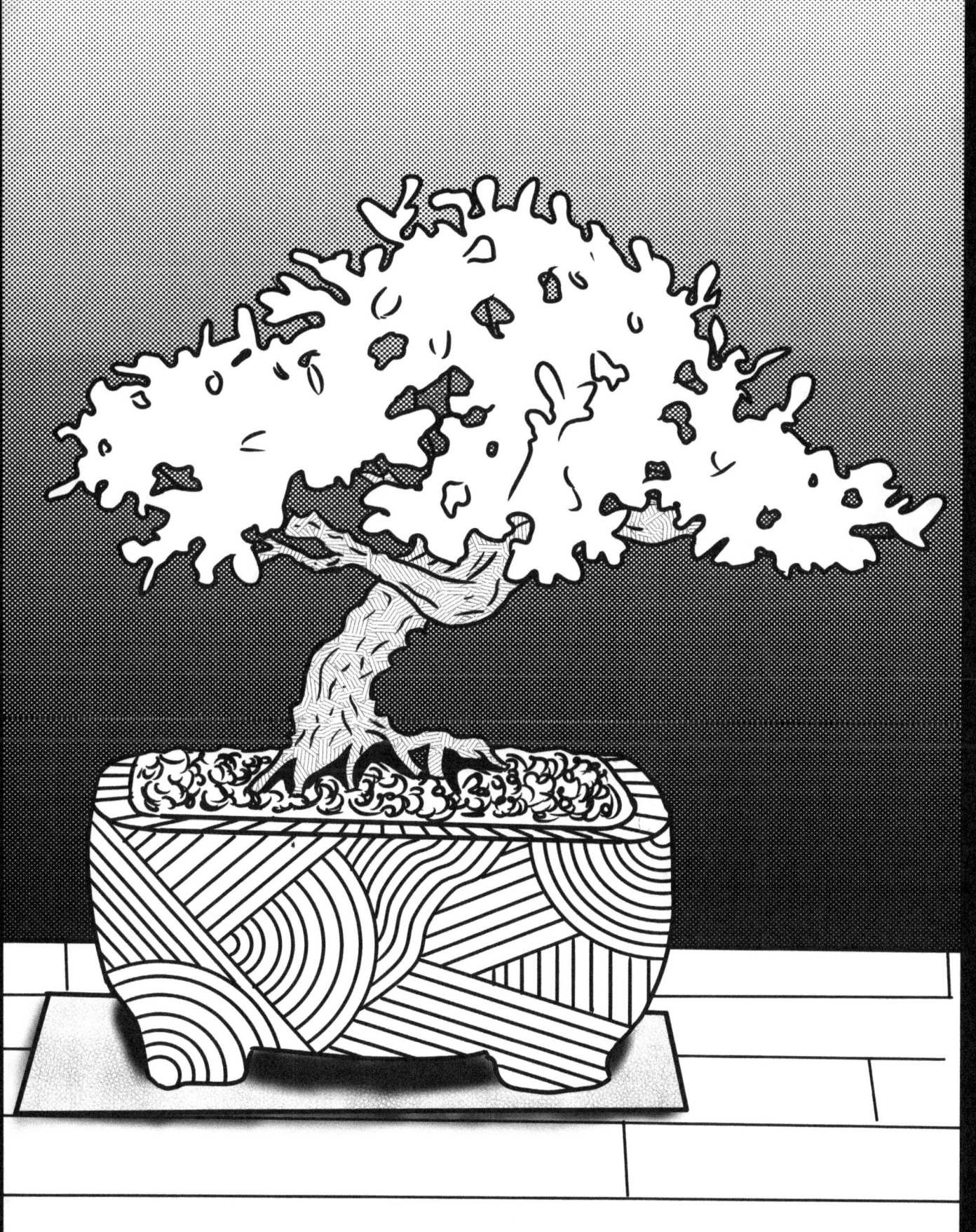

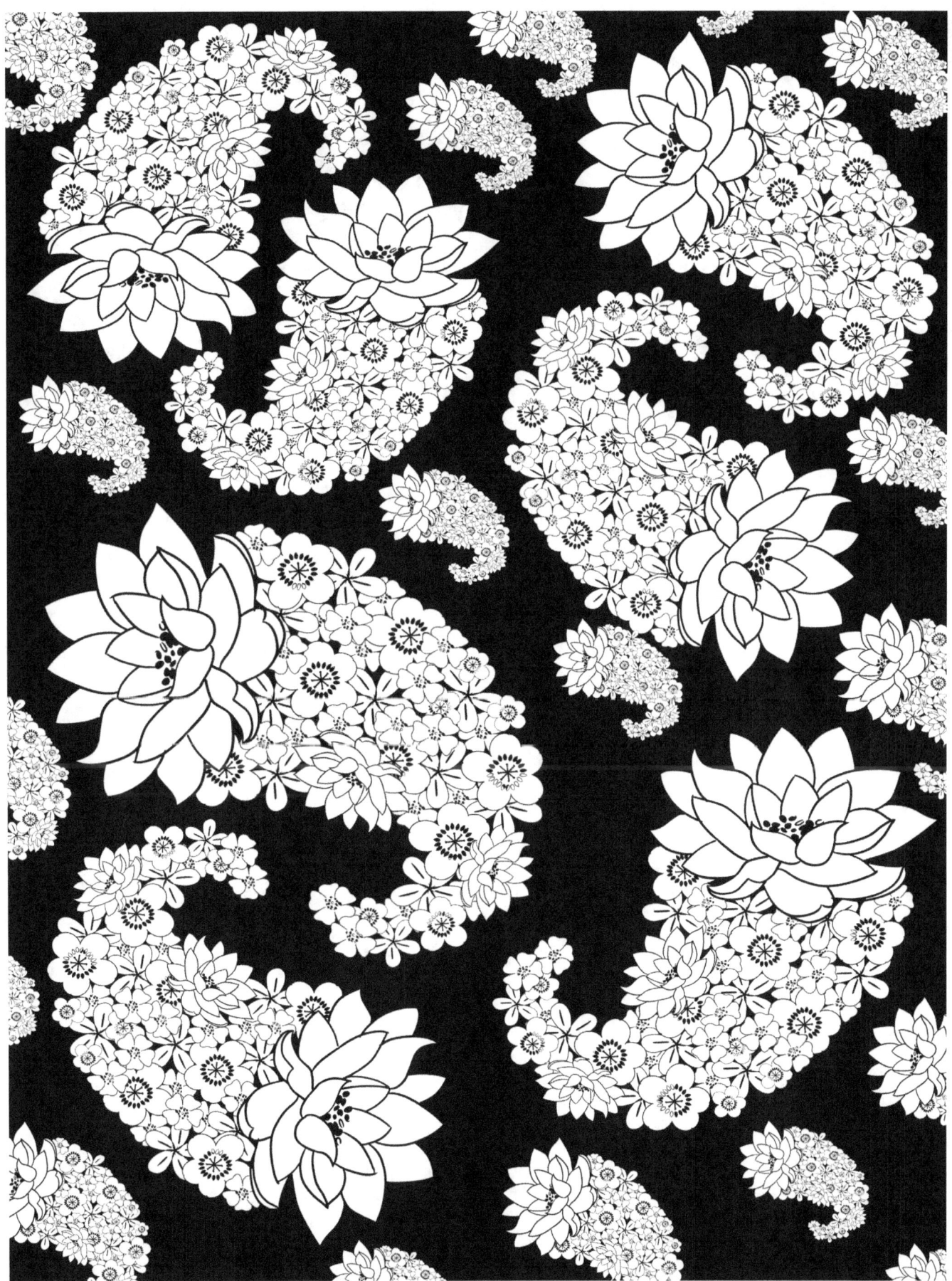

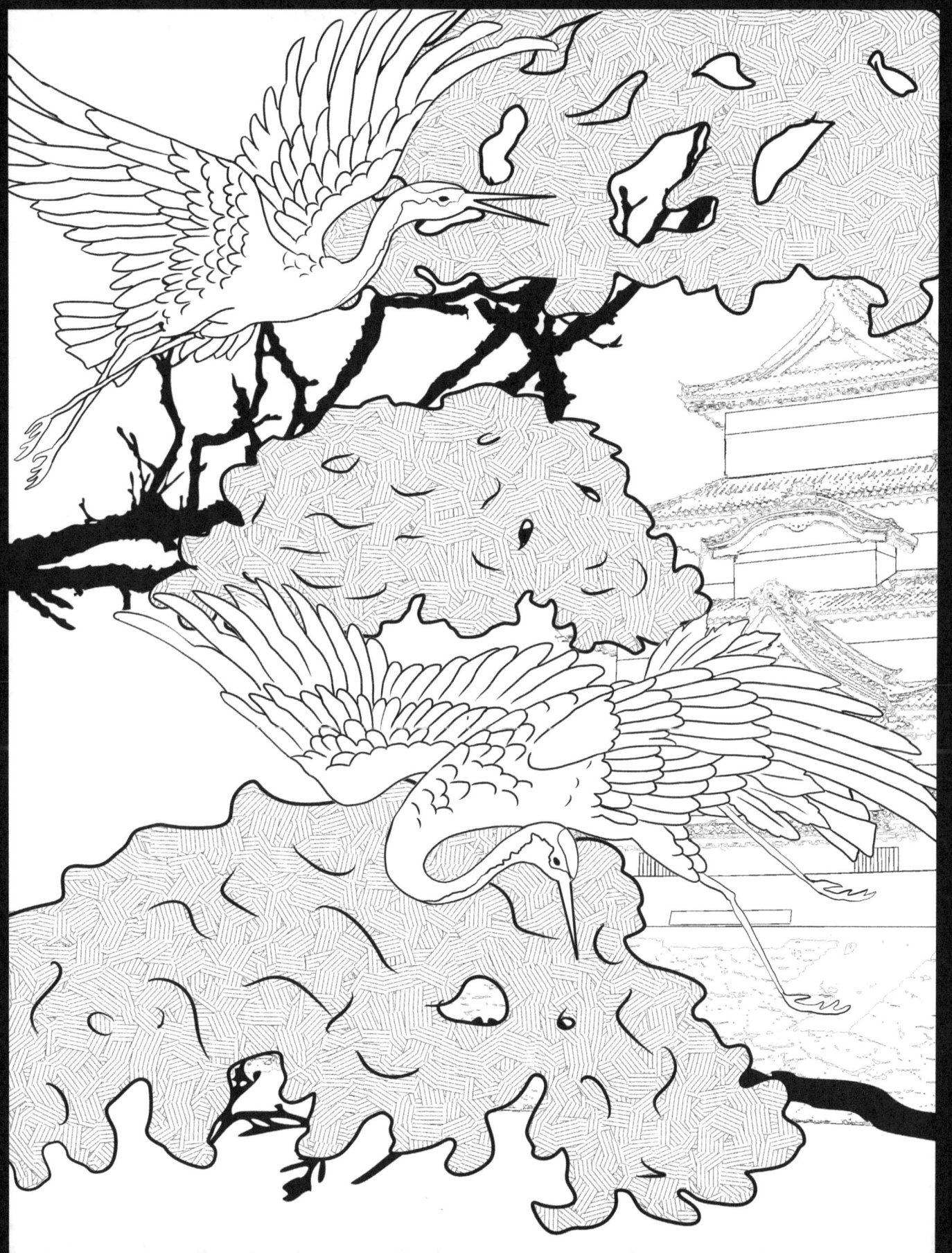

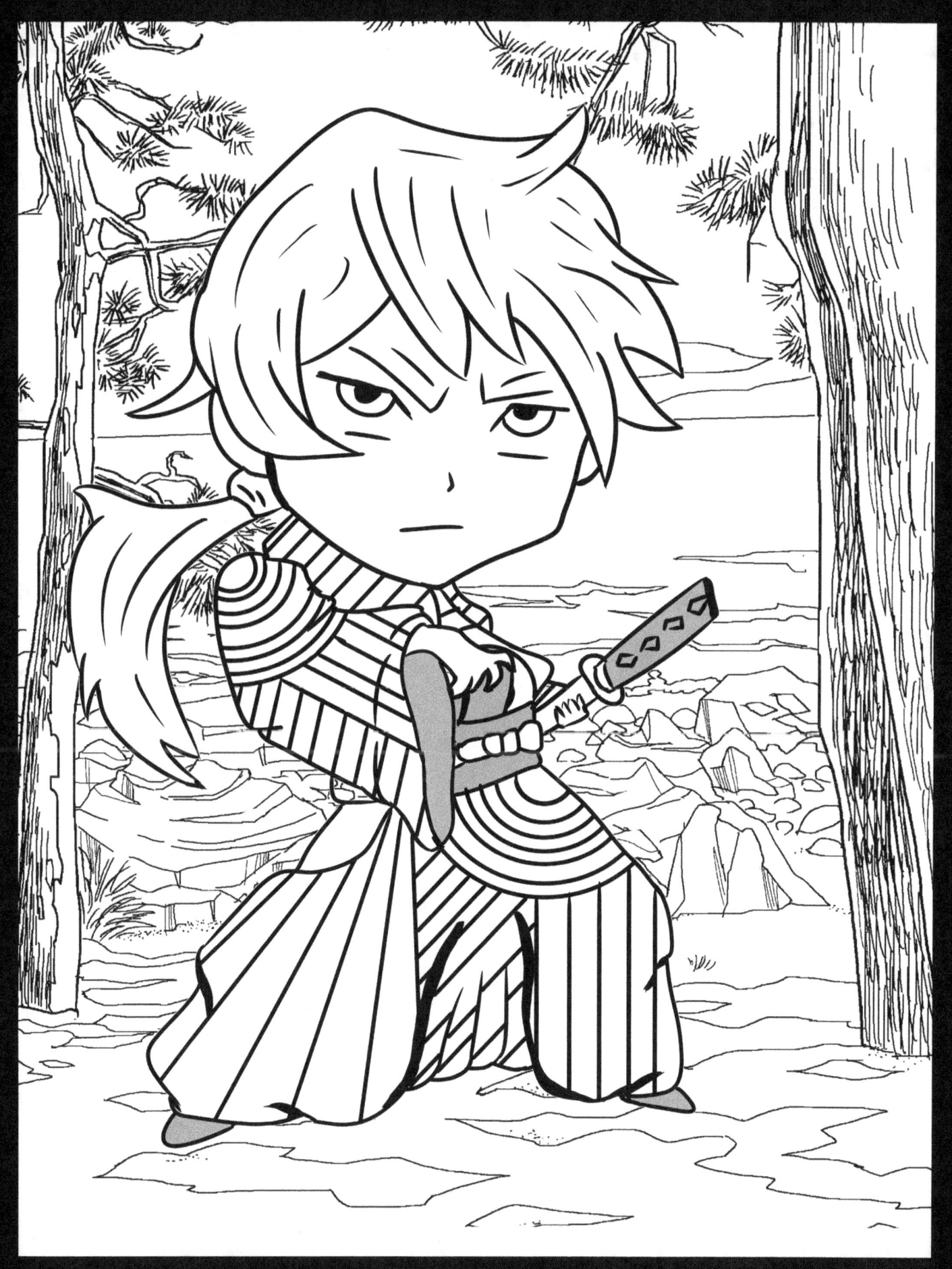

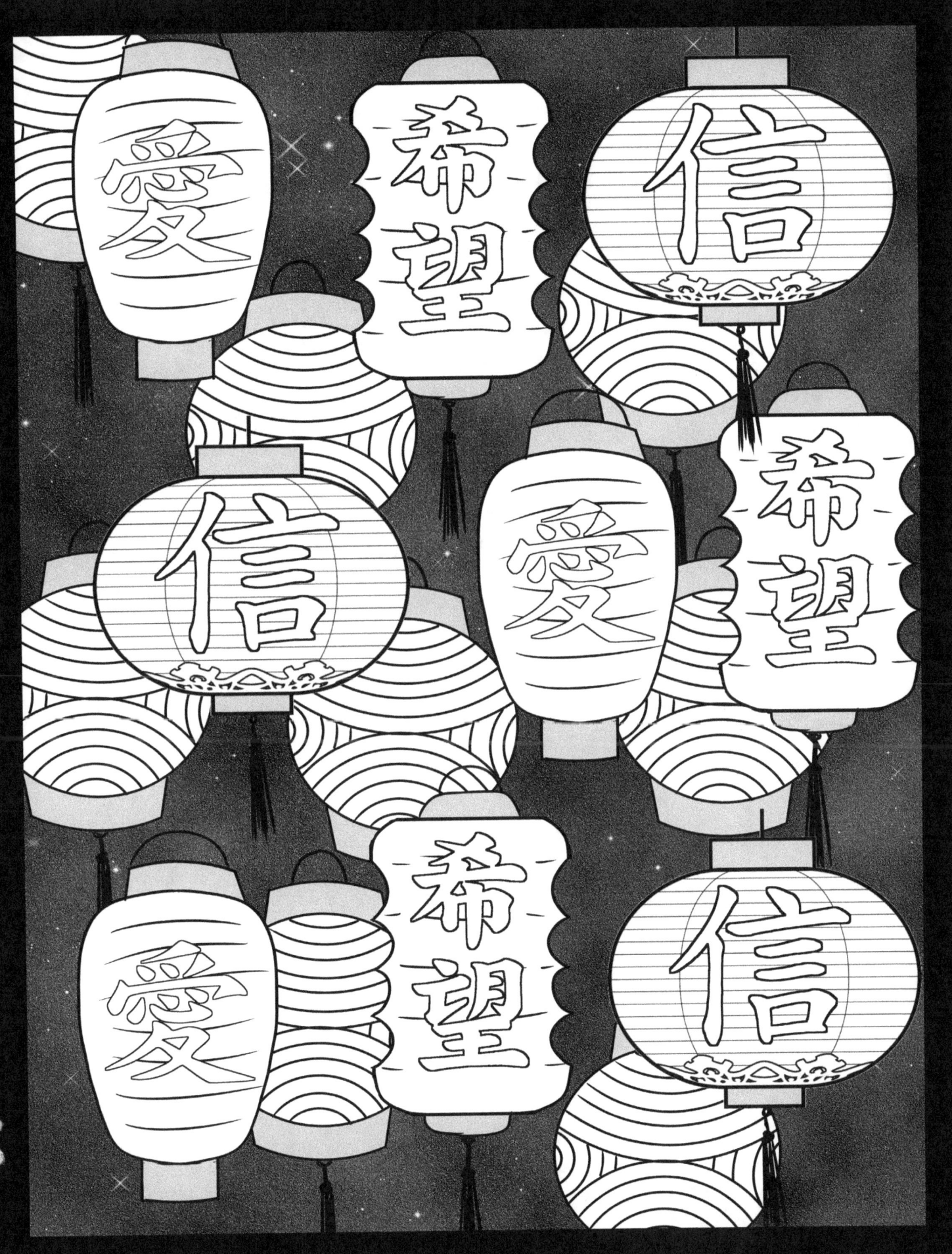

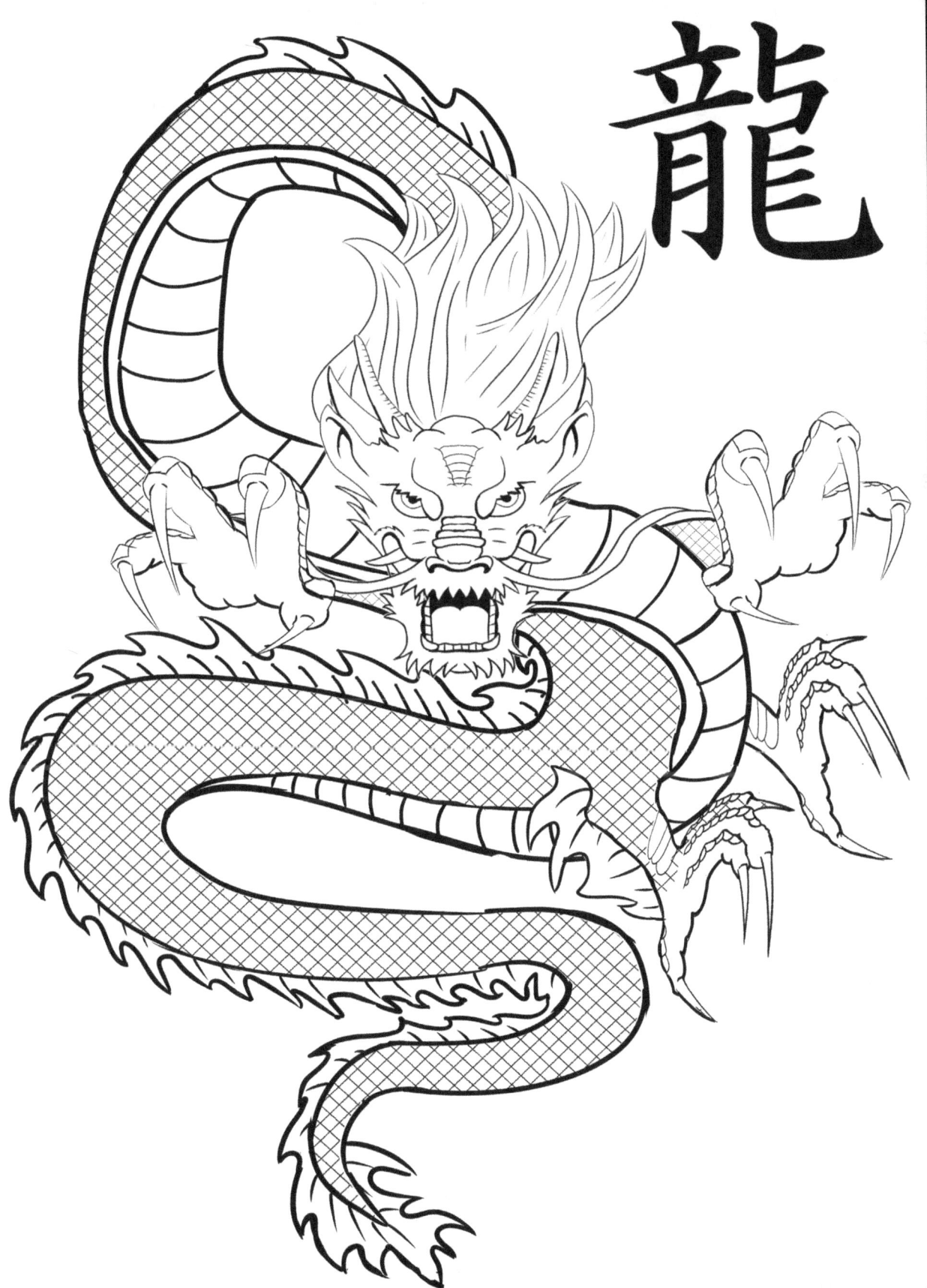

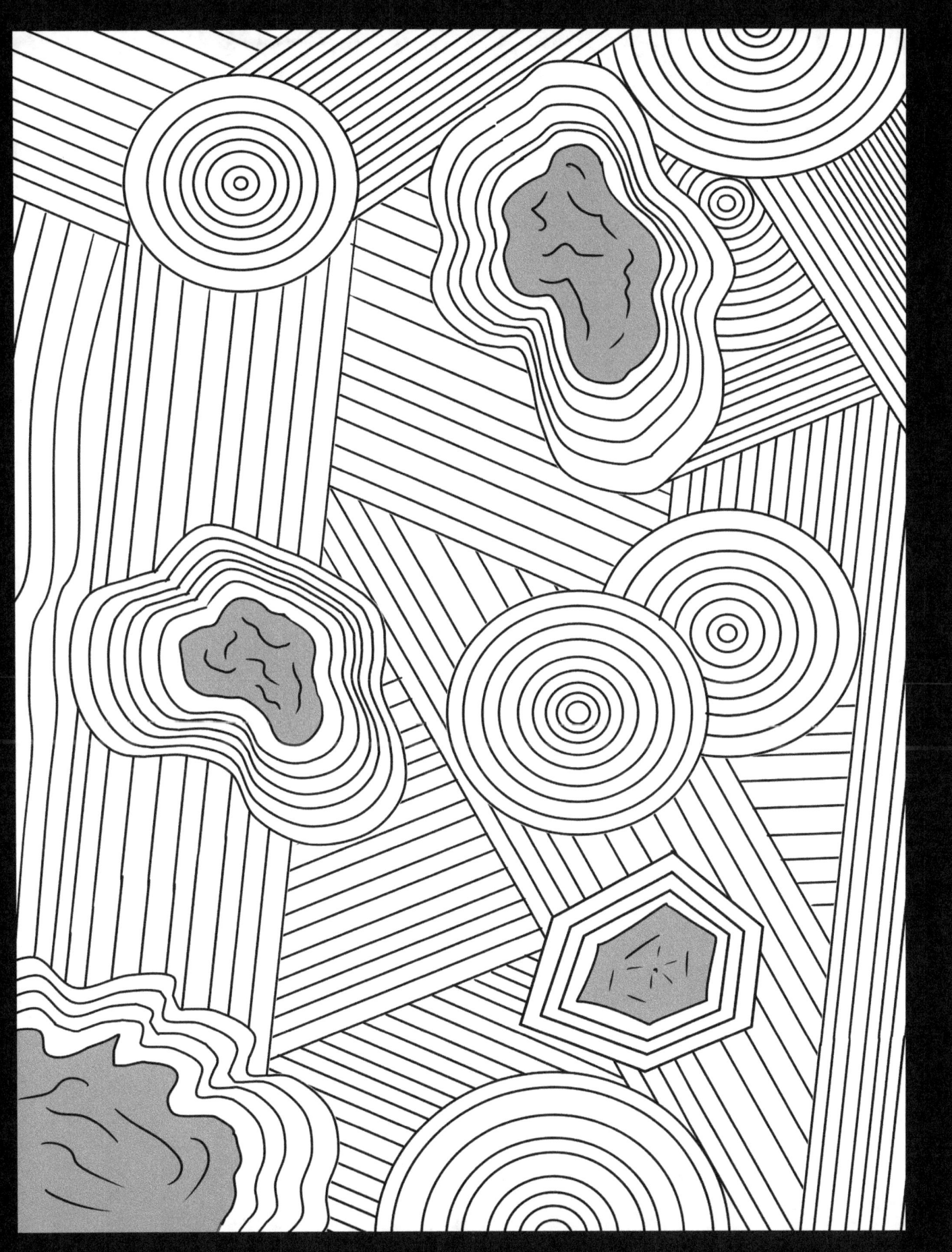

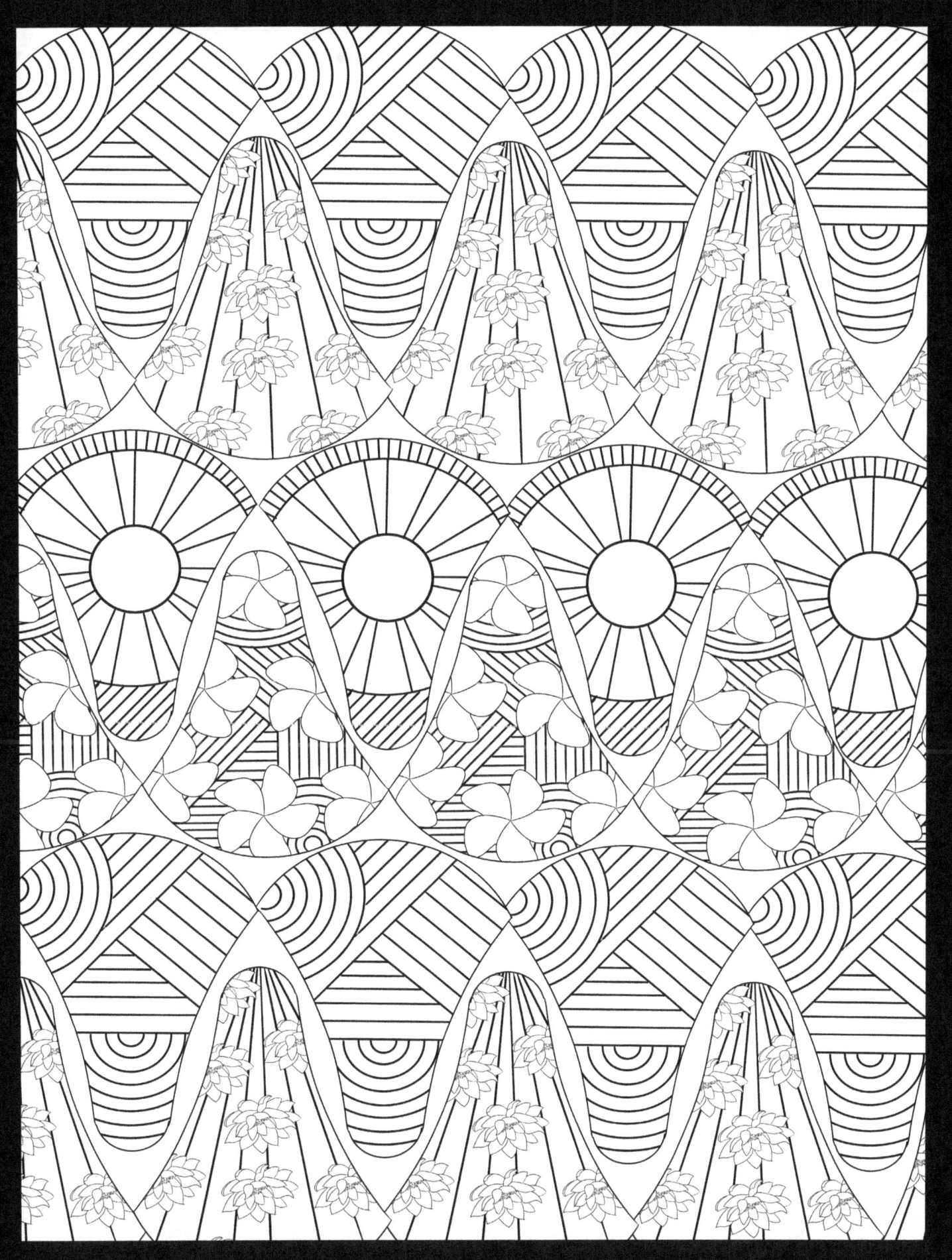

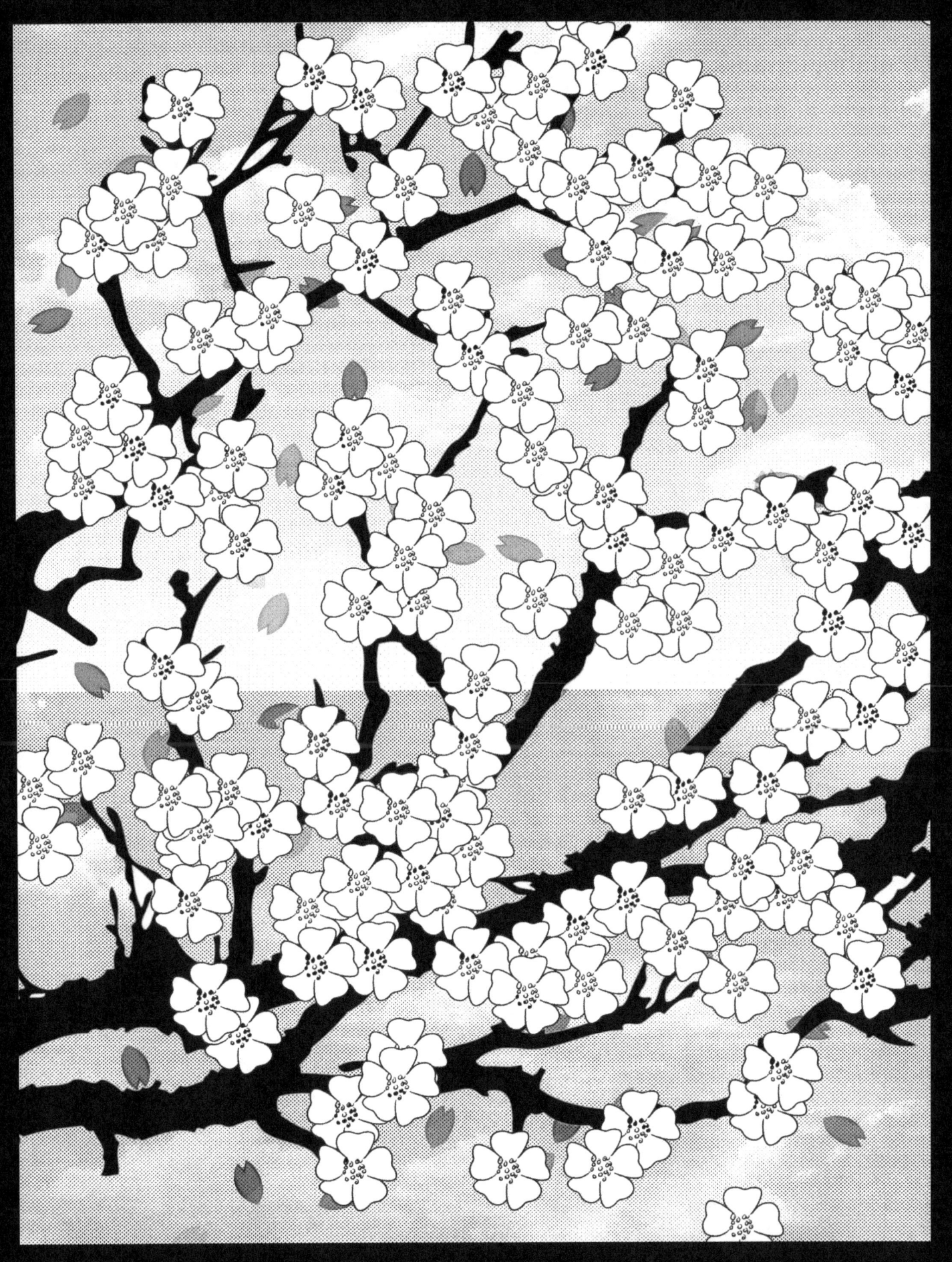

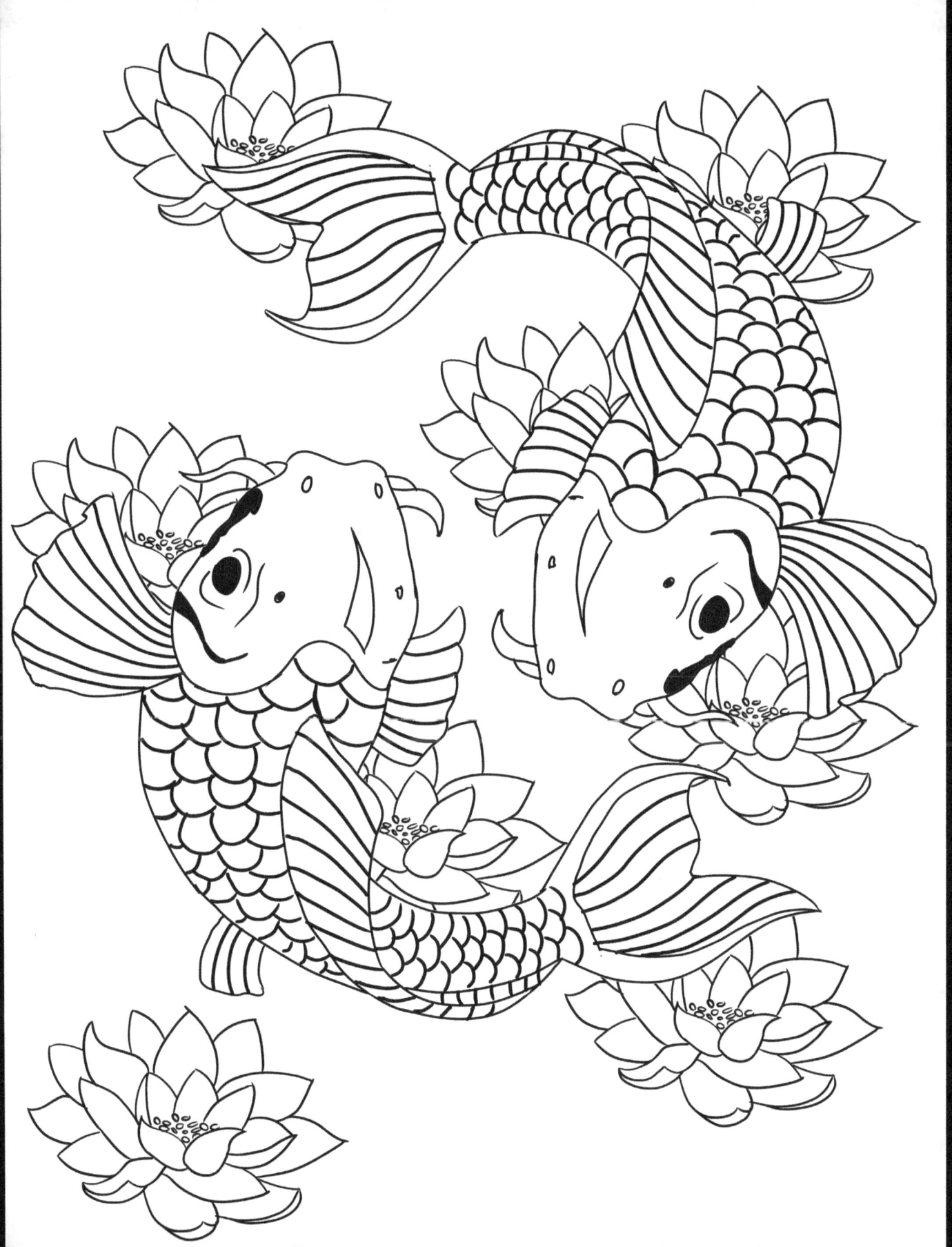

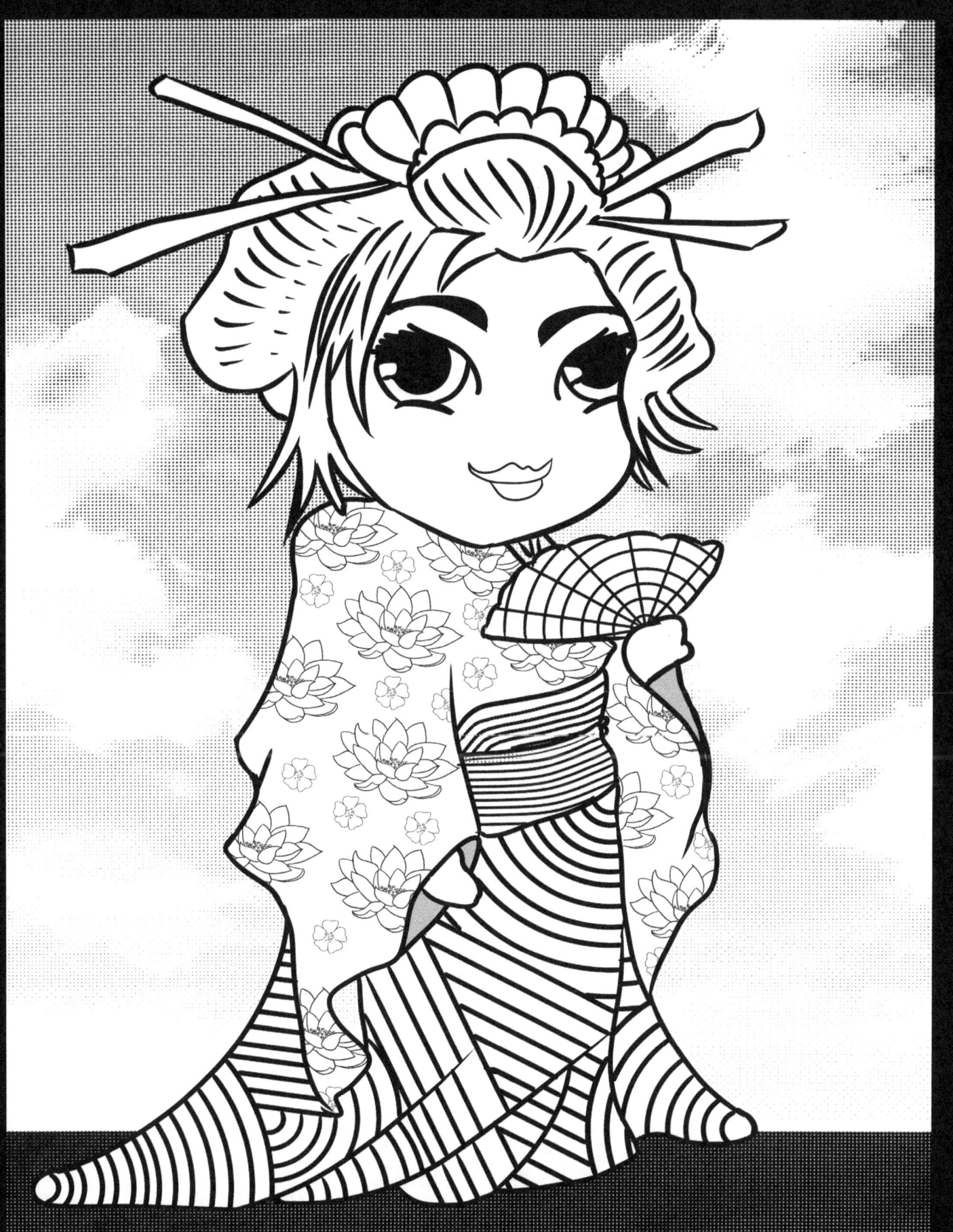

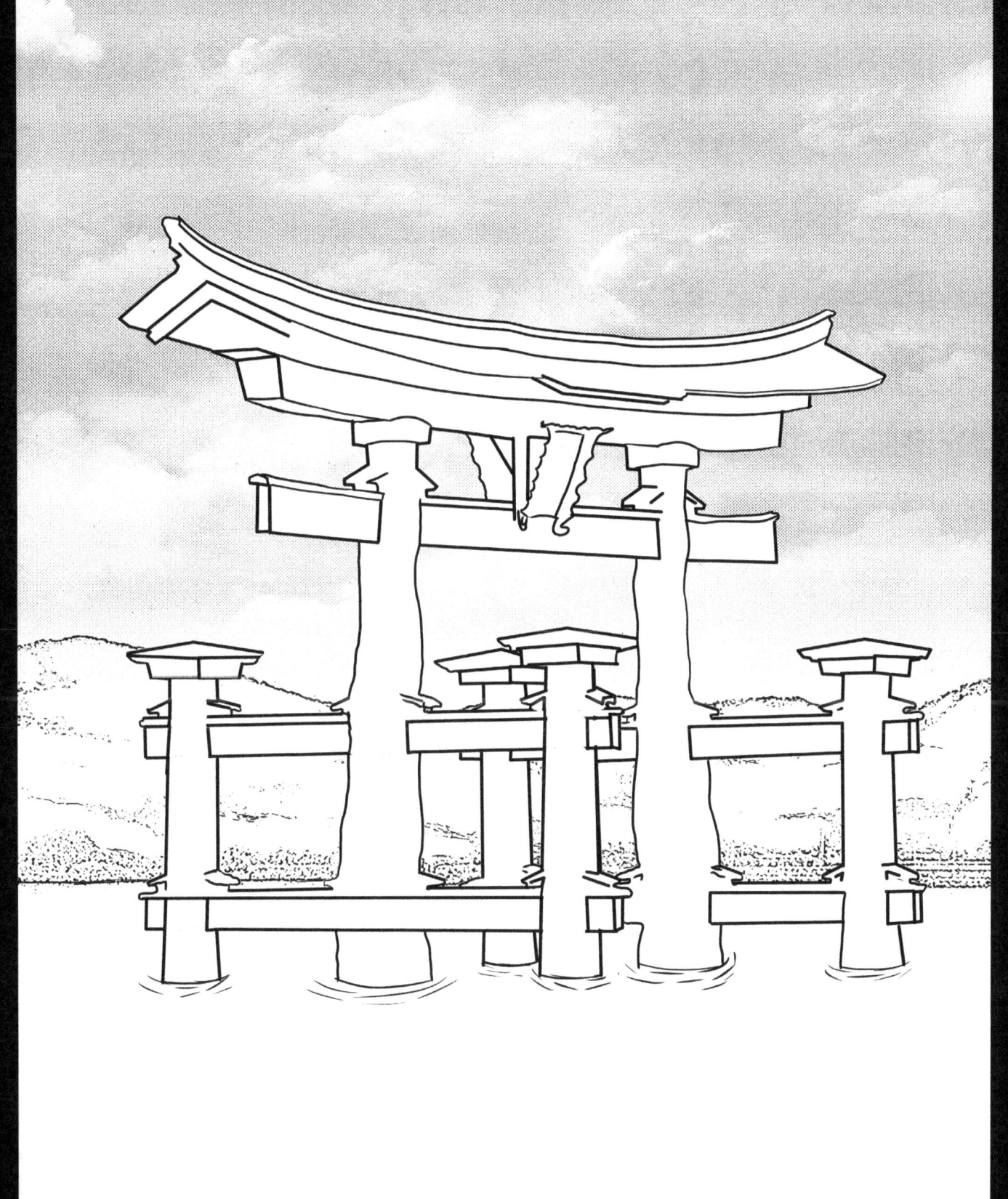

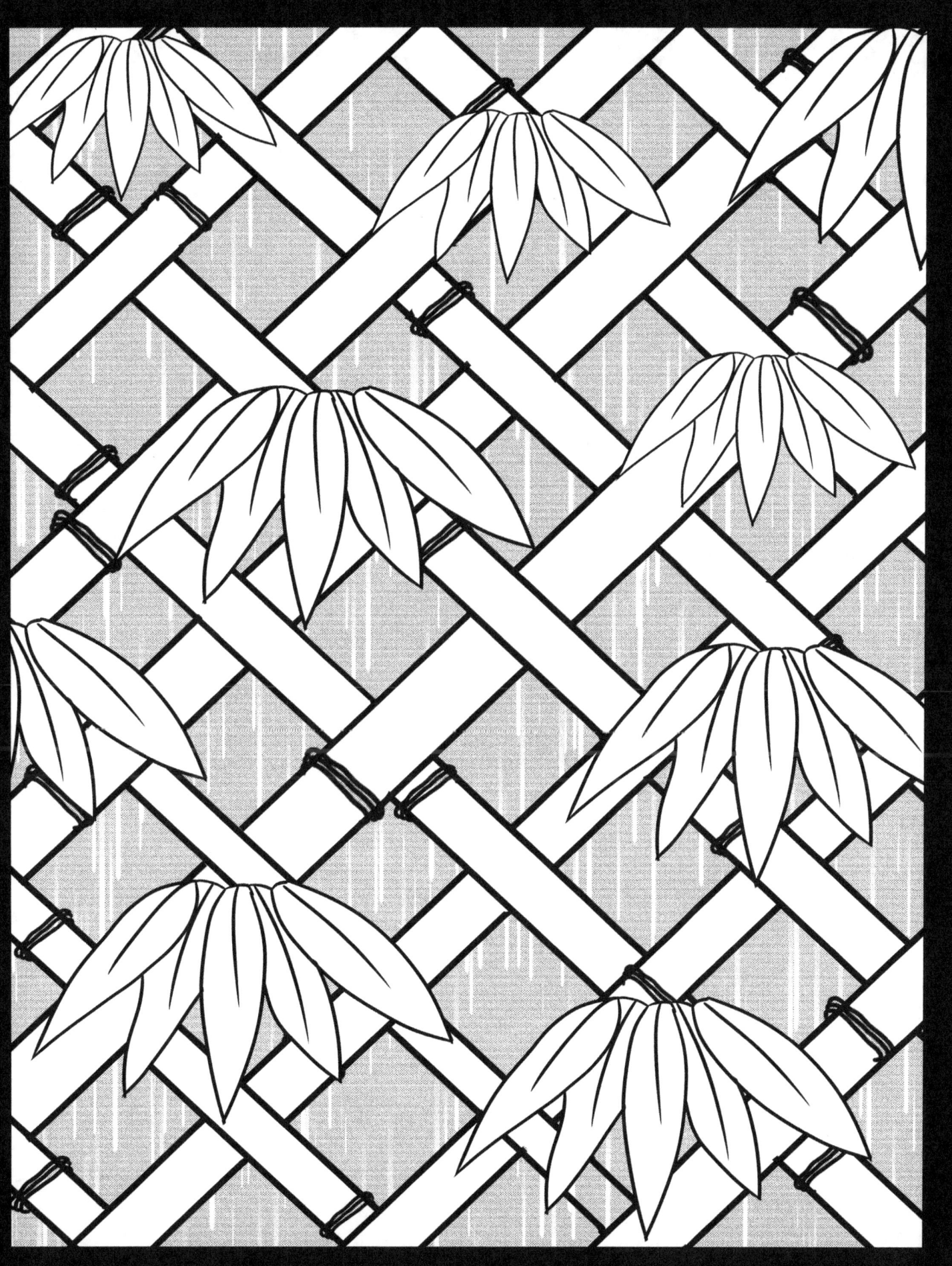

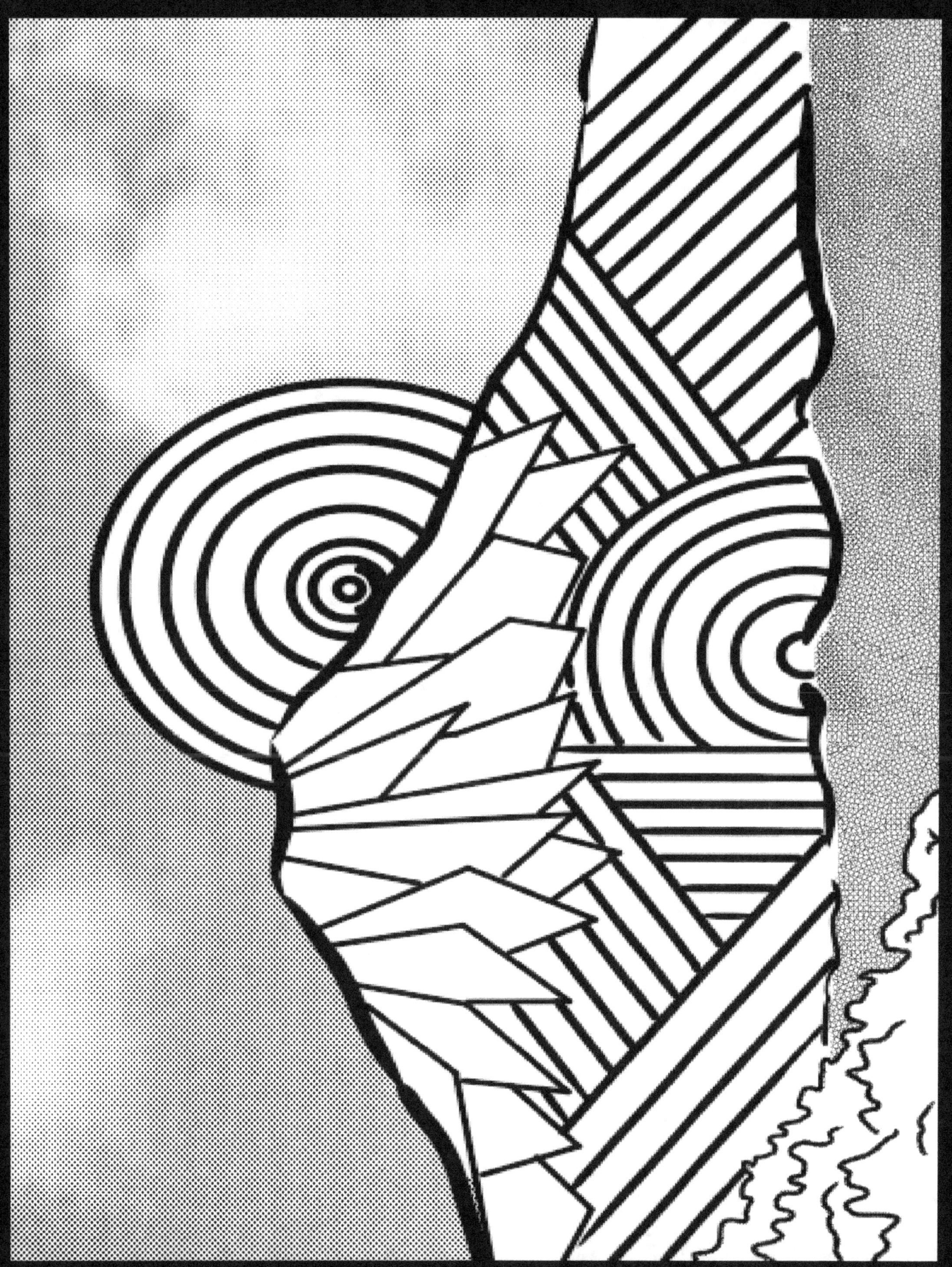

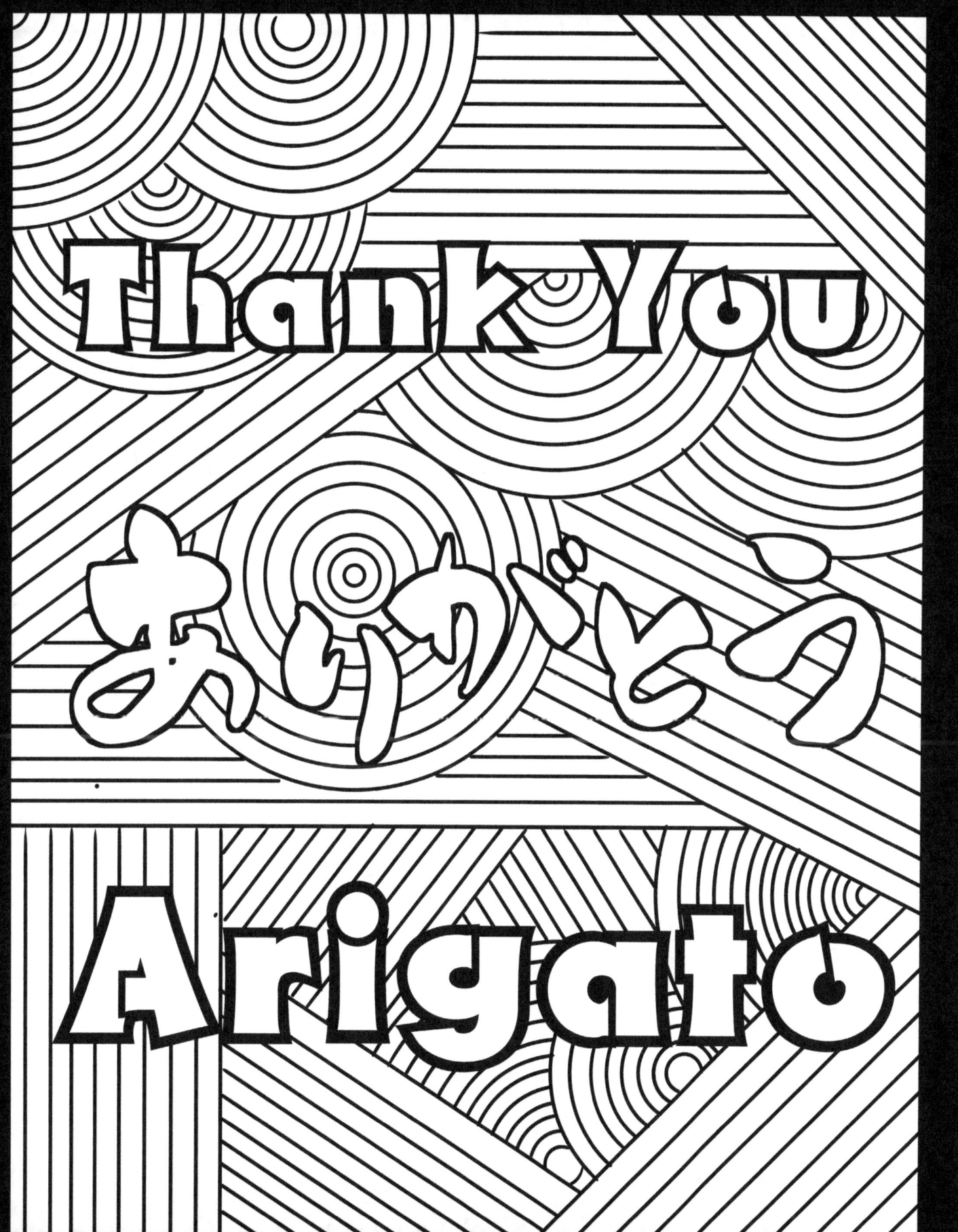